序文
　　　　最初に、ありがとうございます。あなたかこの本
を手にとってくれたことが、私にはとても意味のあること
なのです。たとえこれが最後のページであっても、ありが
とう。
この本は私がスケッチブックに書き溜めた作品でできて
います。想像力溢れる友人の作品一点をのぞいた全て
が私のイマジネーションから生み出されたものです。
私は人が感じる独自の解釈を尊重する為、この本では
作品の意味や閃きを敢えて解説しないようにしていま
す。
最後に、これからも私は可能な限り創造し続けますの
で、決してこれが最初で最後の出版物でない事をお伝
えします。

PREFACE

　　　　First and foremost, Thank you. It means a lot to me that
you took a moment to view this book. Regardless if this page is as
far as you decide to turn, I still thank you. The artwork featured
within this edition are compositions taken from a sketchbook I
had filled. The following visuals were all from my imagination
except, of course, a single entry by another creative friend. Unlike
various artist, I respectfully refuse to explain and decipher
meanings and inspirations behind each piece. My reasoning for
this is because, I do not wish to subtract from any viewer's own
interpretation from what is shown. Be advised, as long as I am
capable of creating art, this is not and will not be the only book
and medium of art to present you, in due time. Again, Thank you

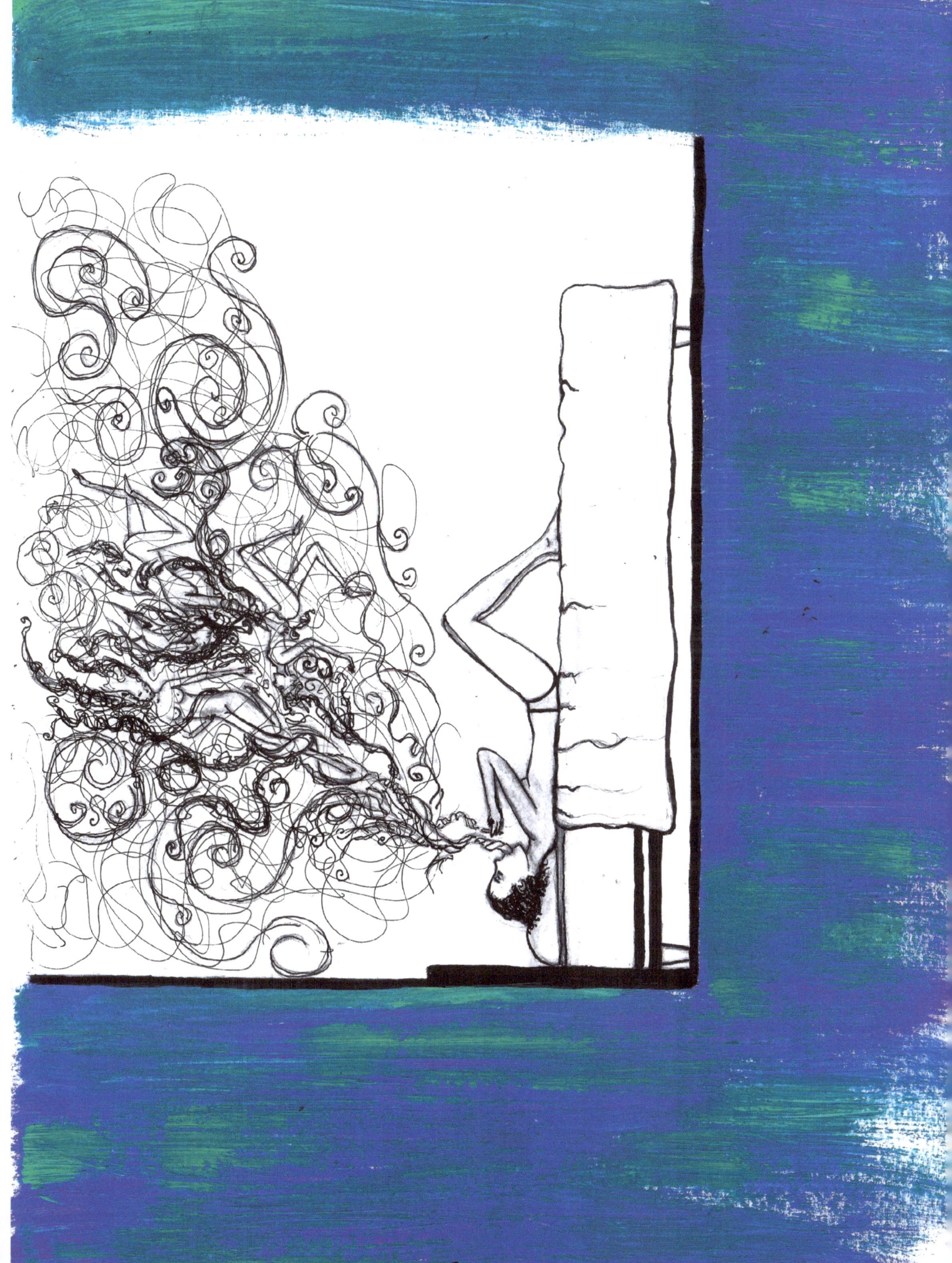

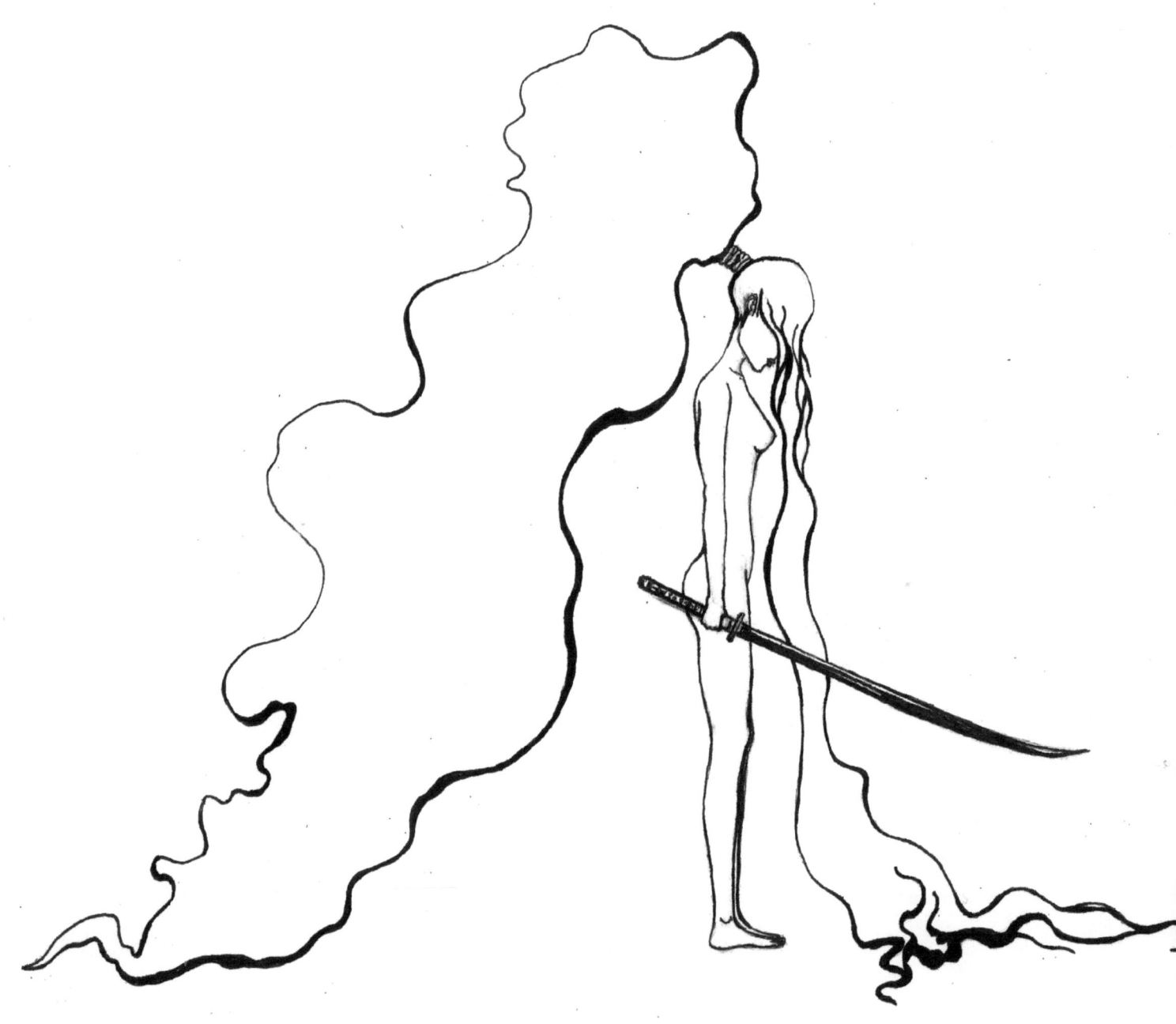

What if this is god?
What if she is god?

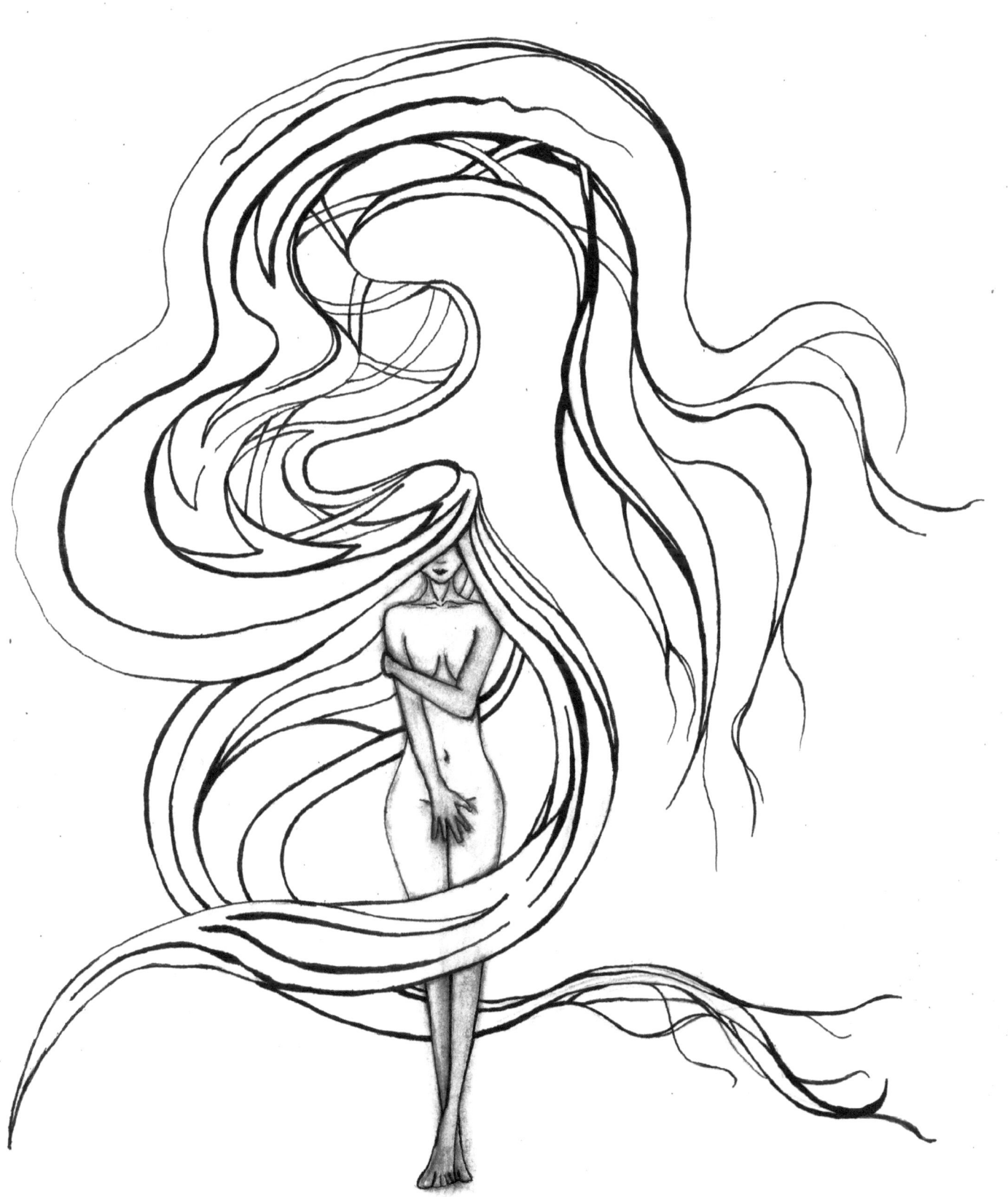

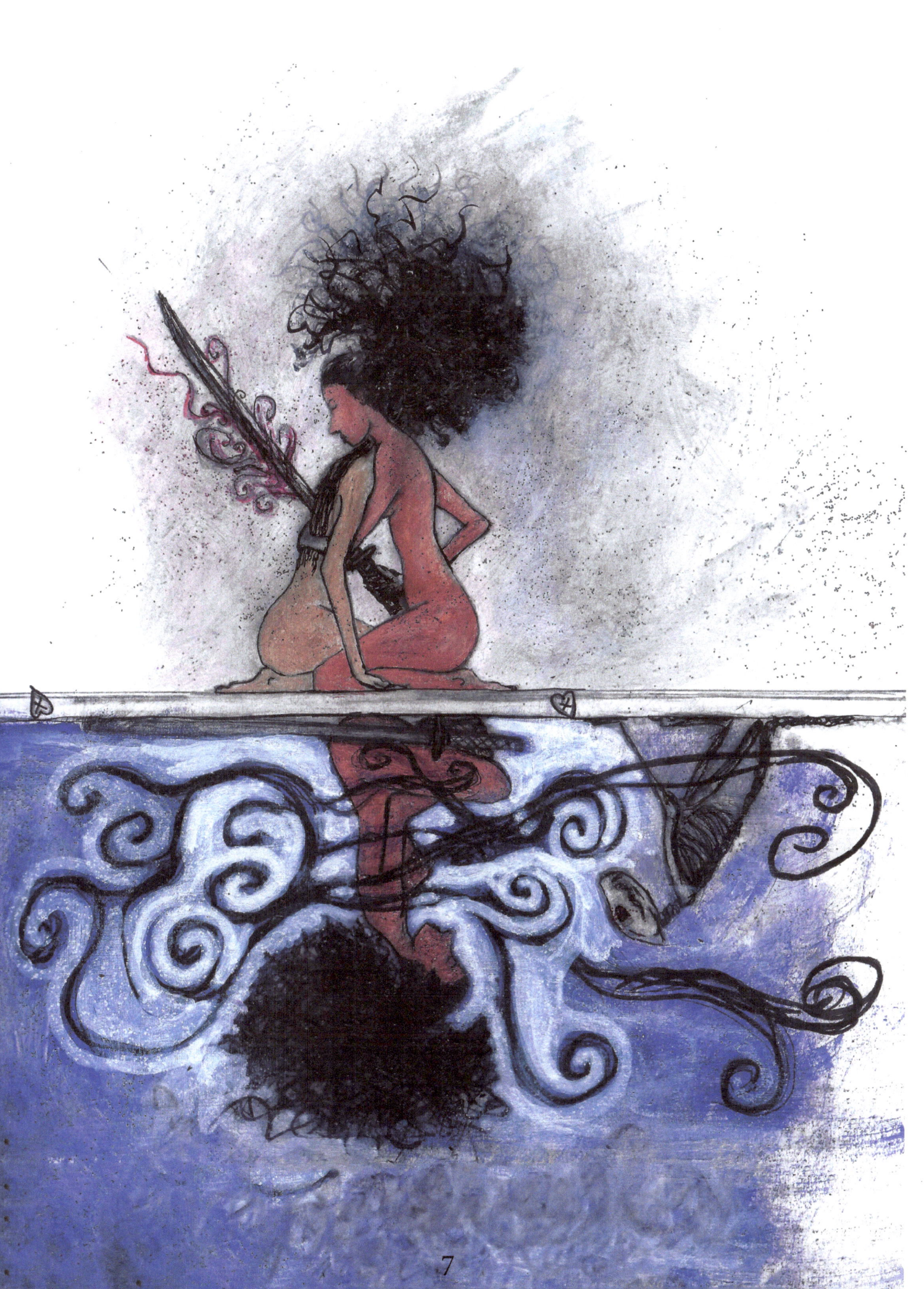

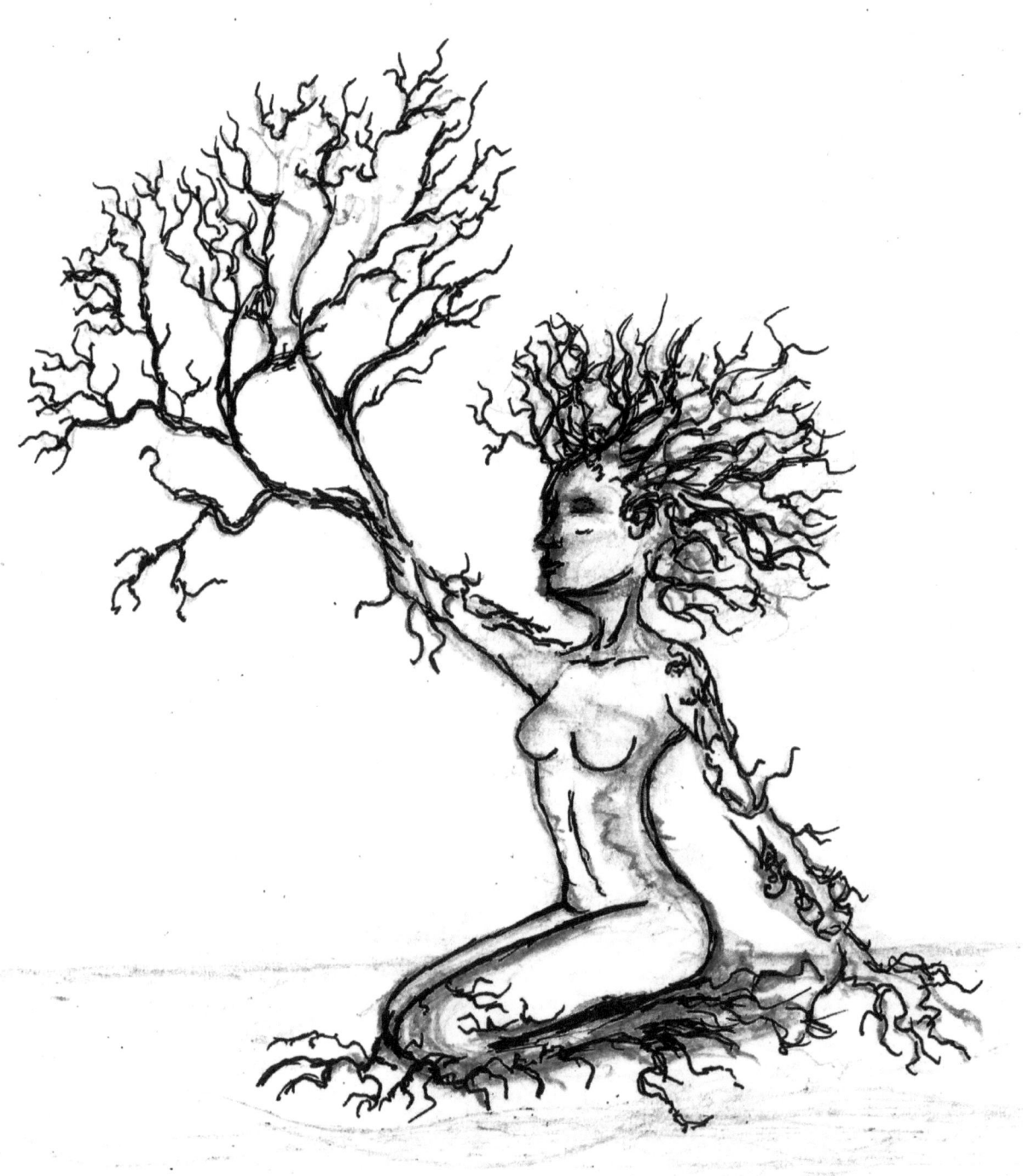

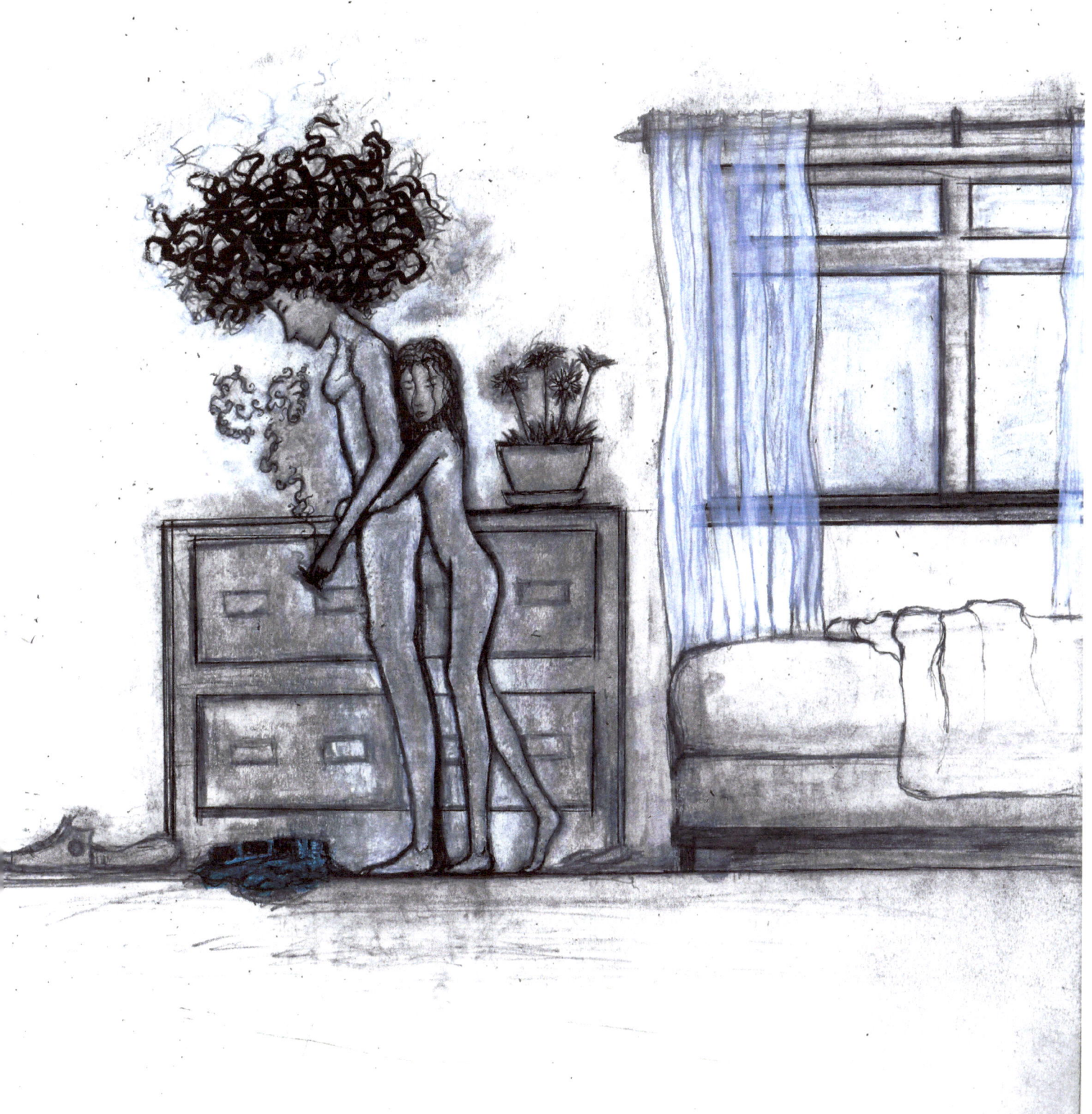

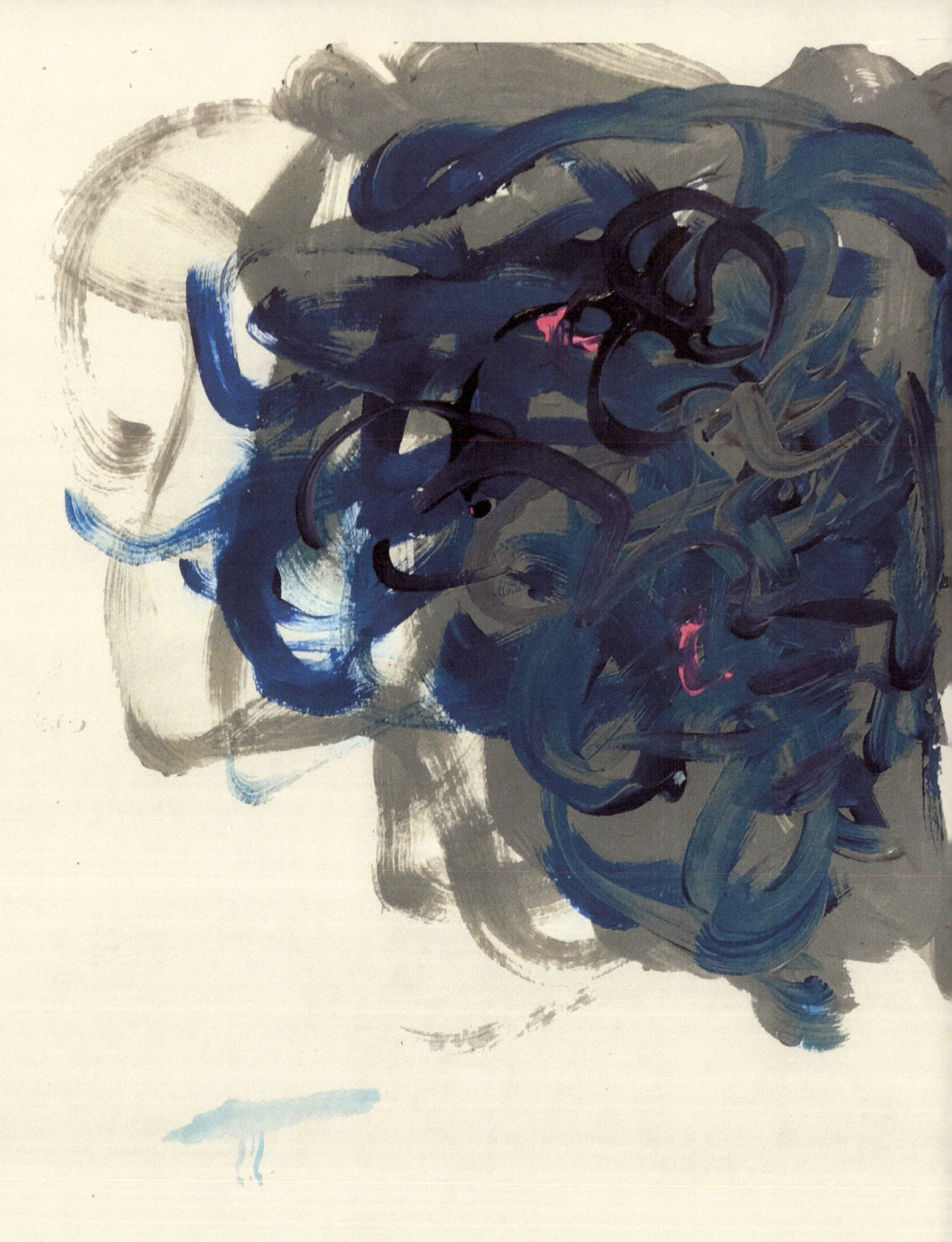

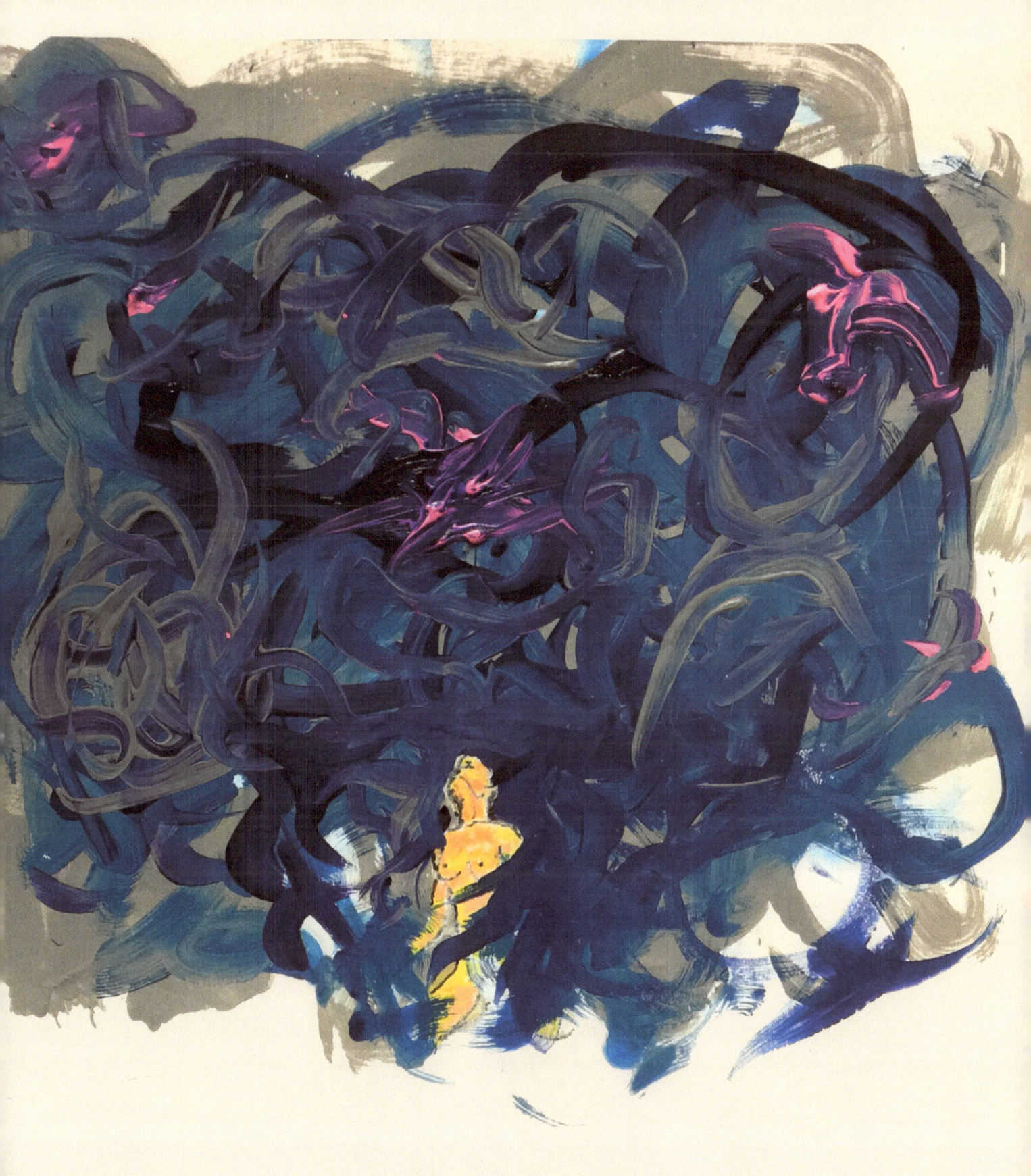

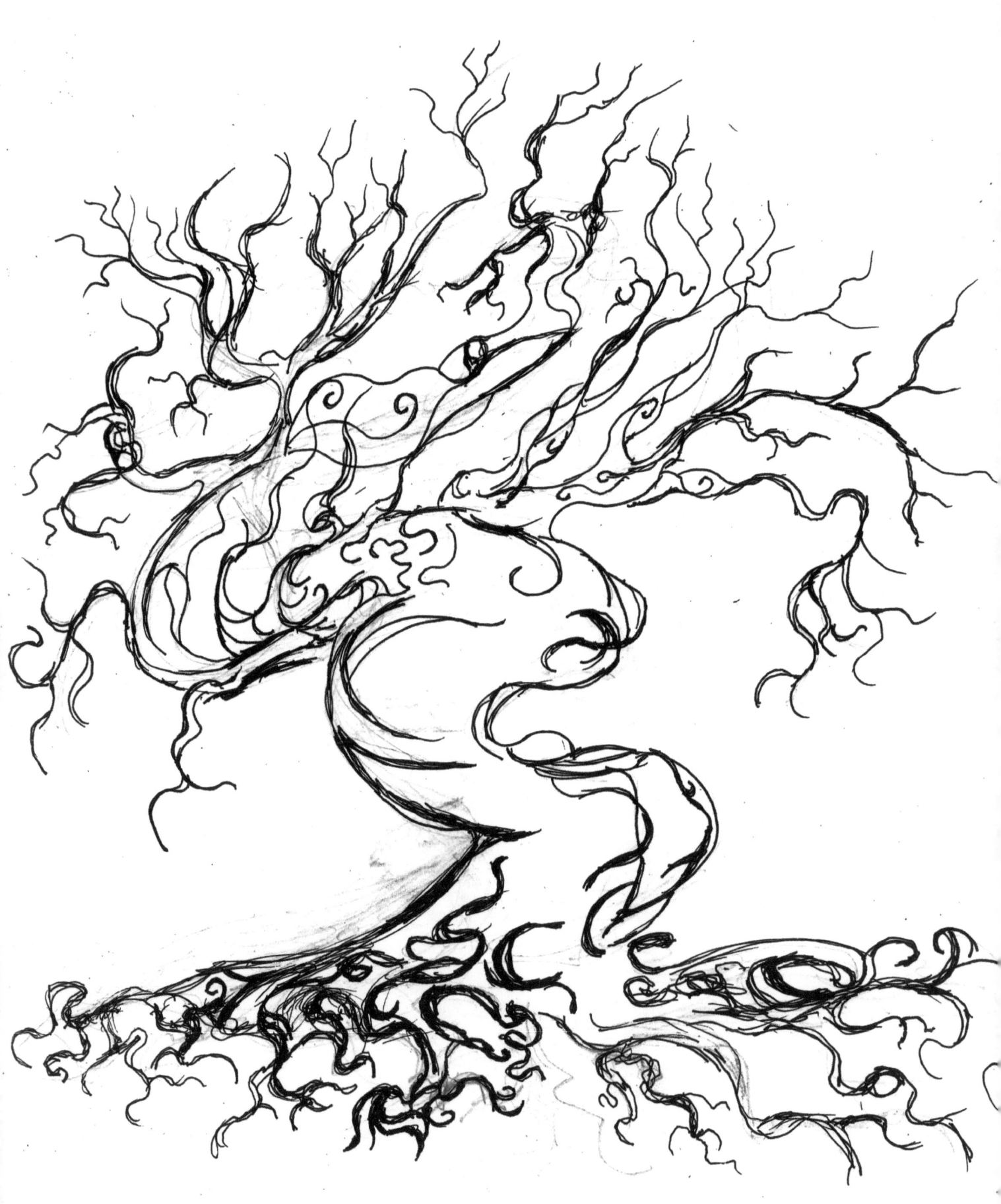

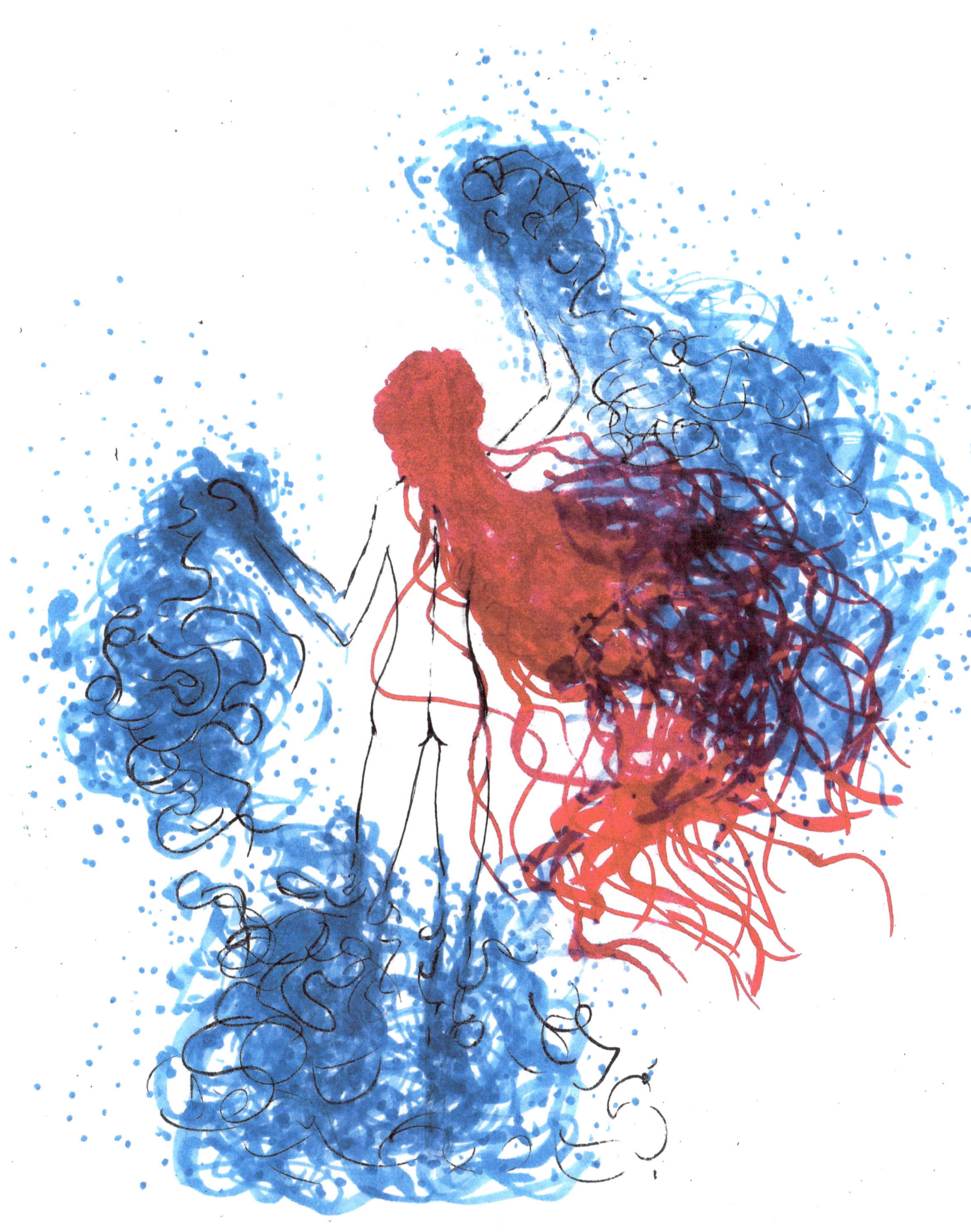

13

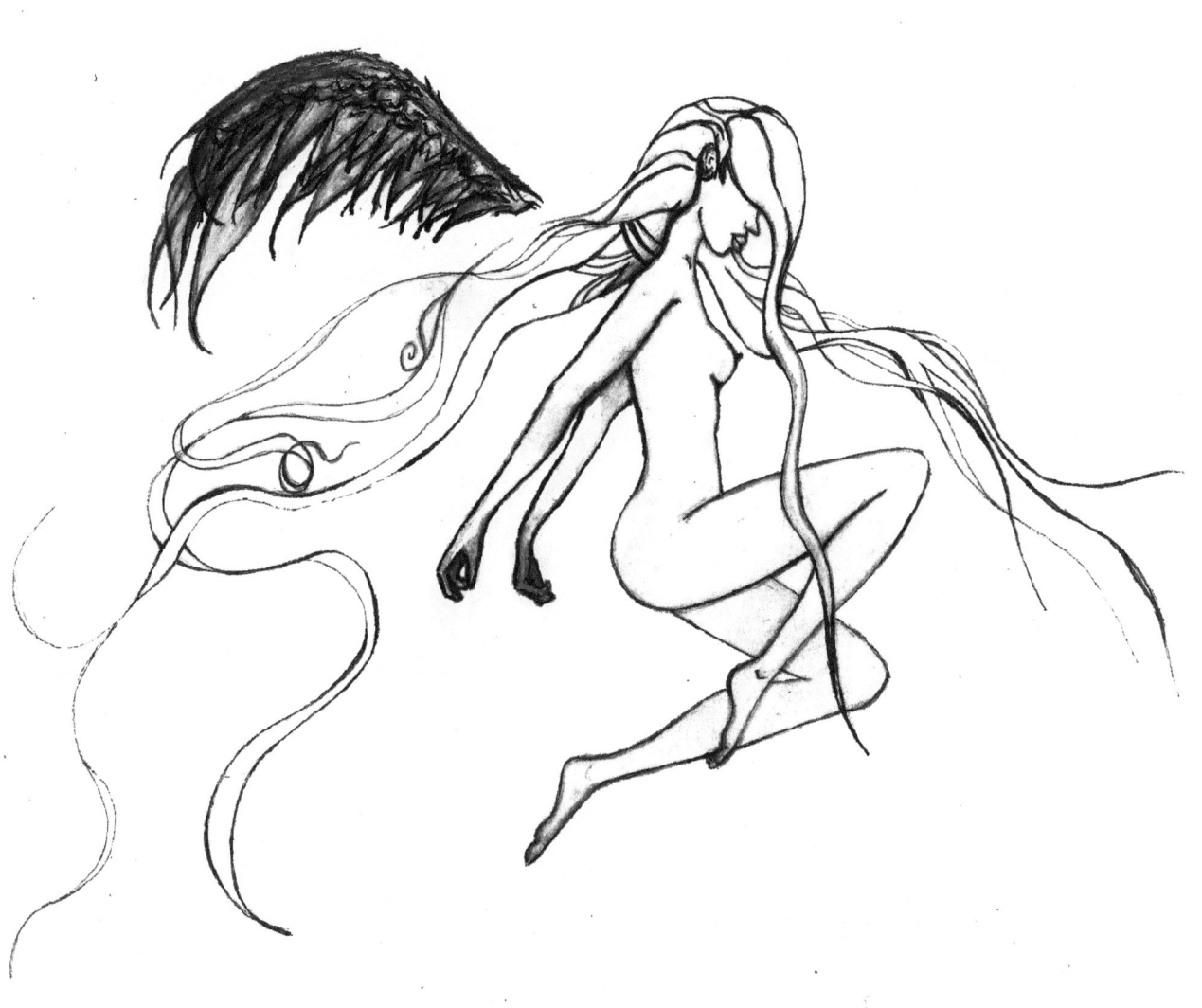

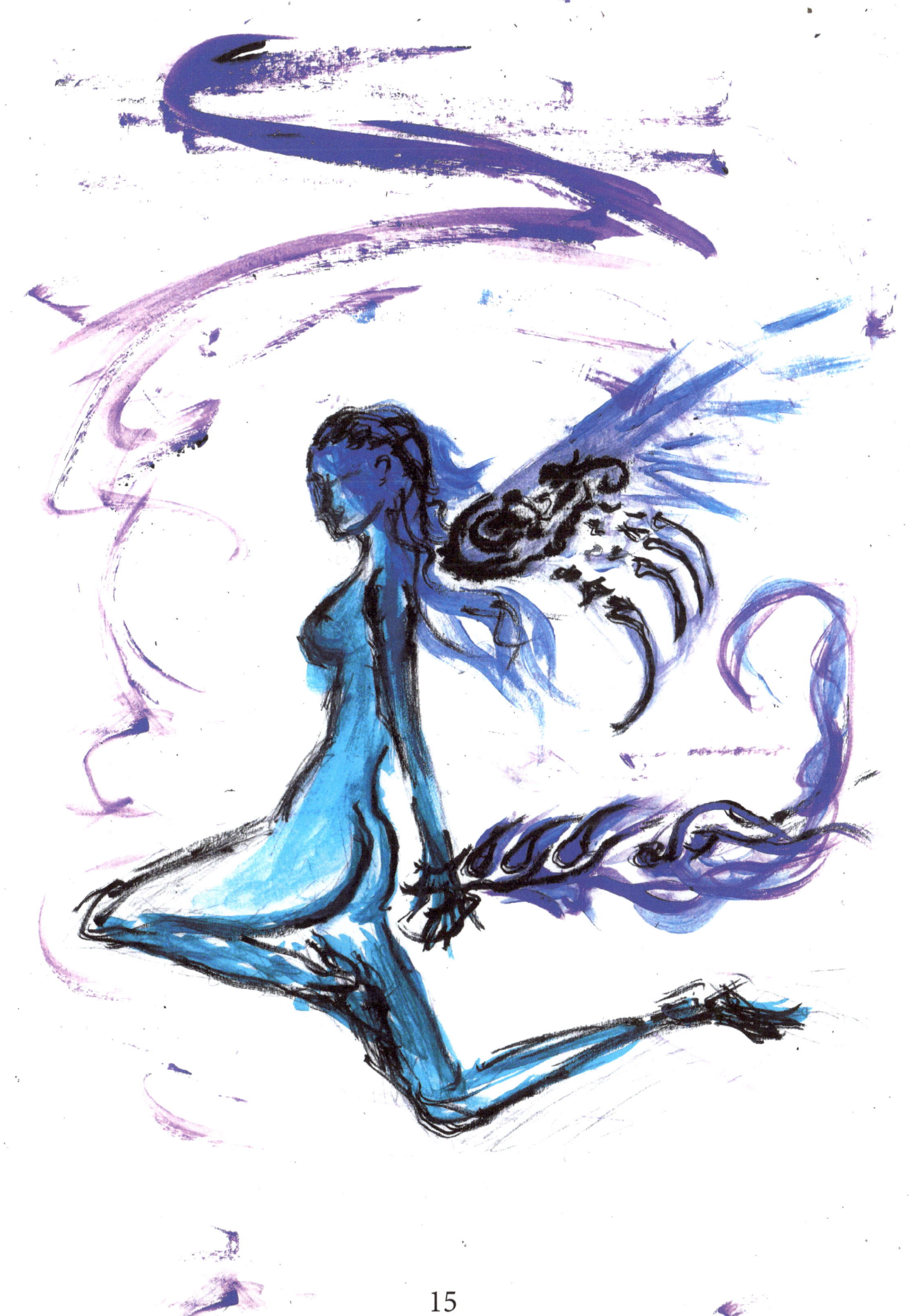

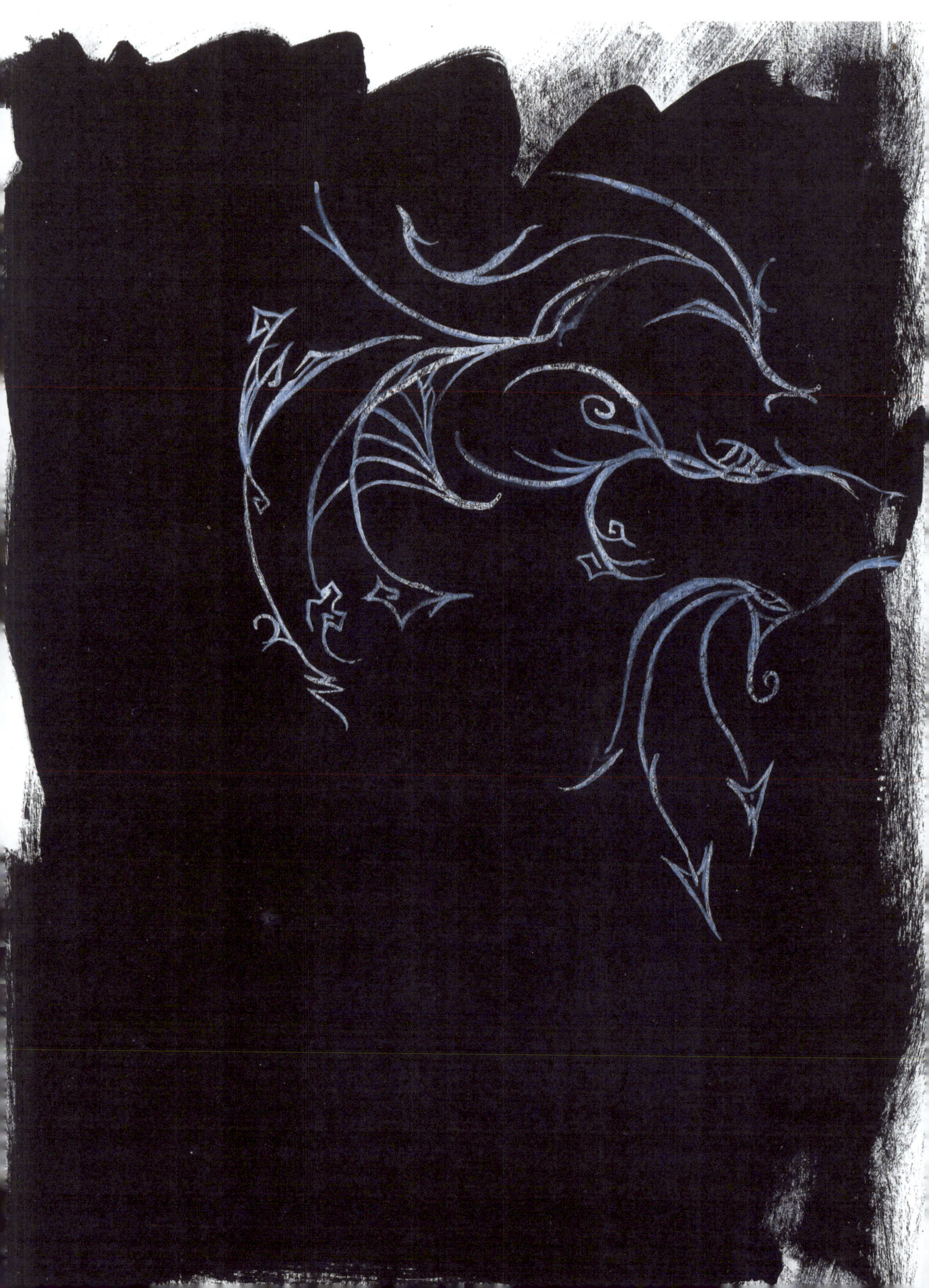

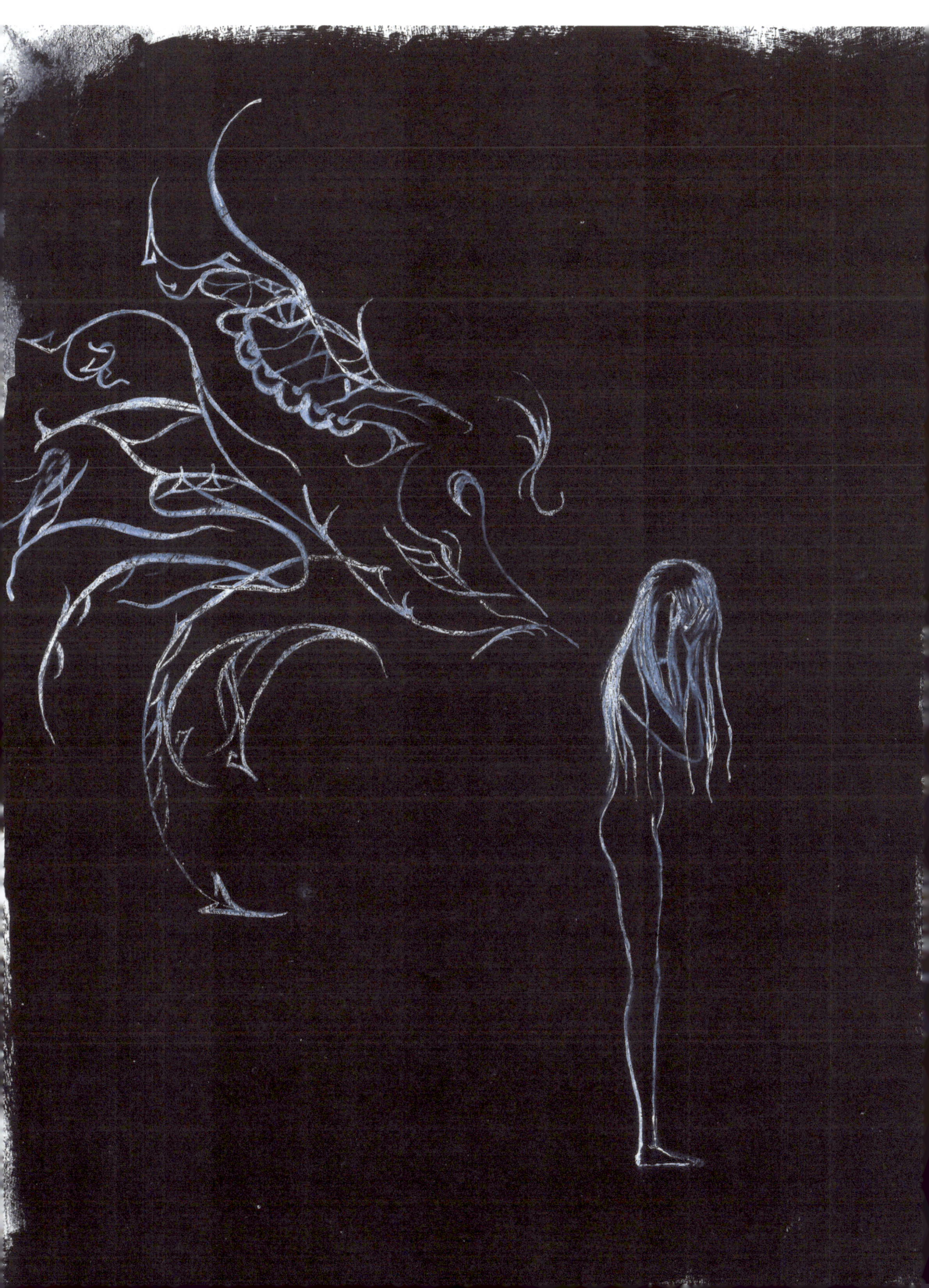

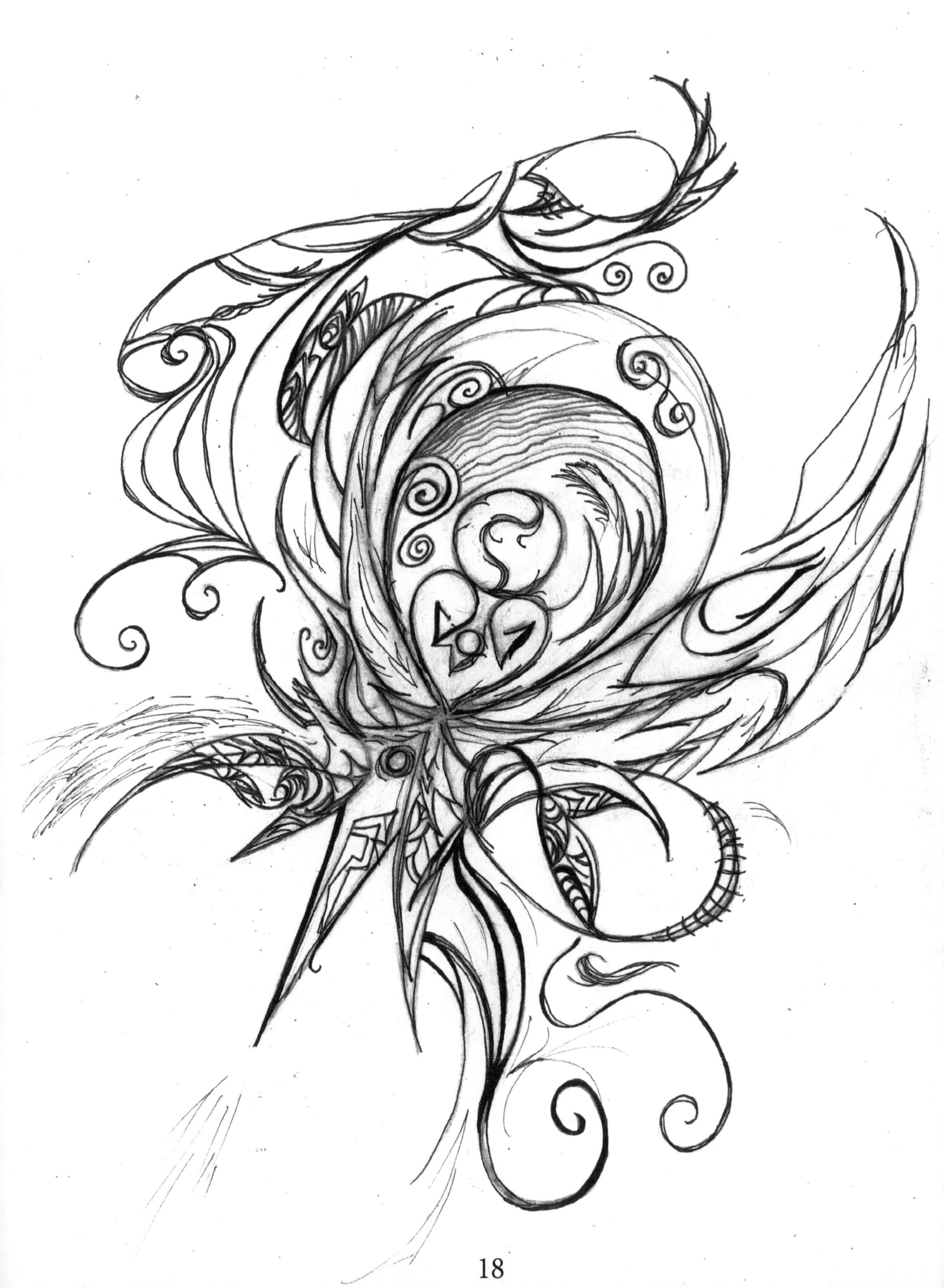

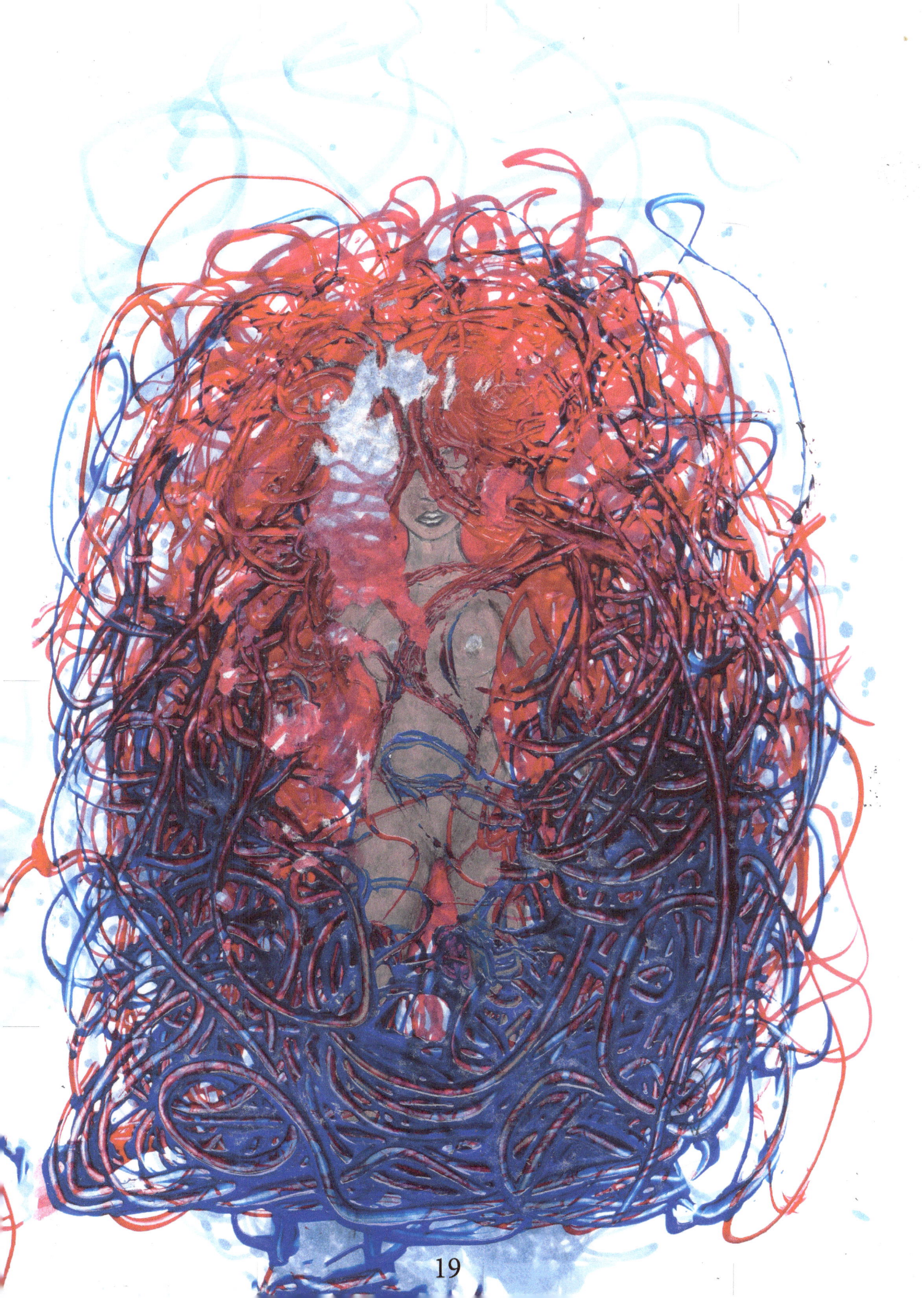

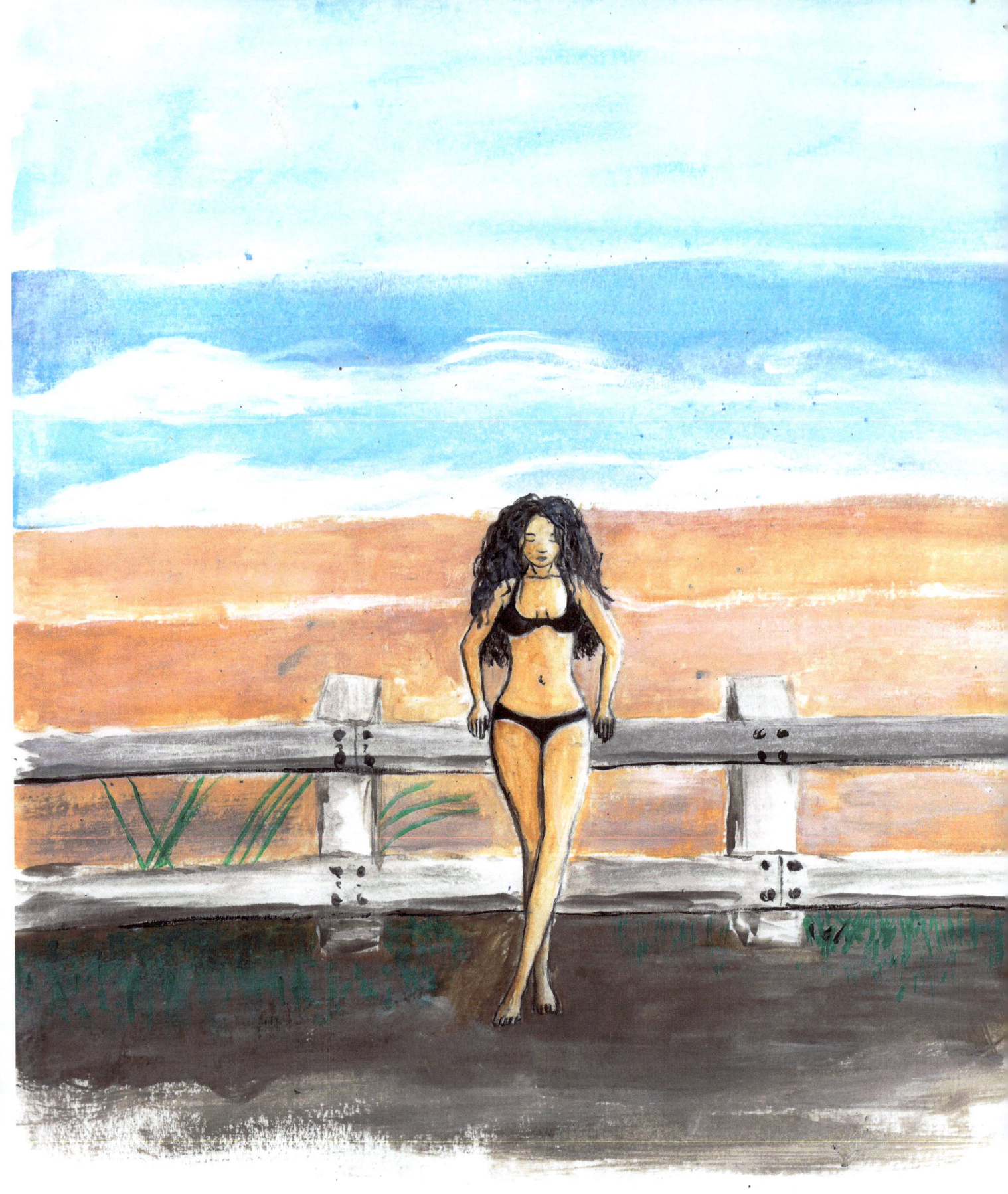

4-5 Jan 2015

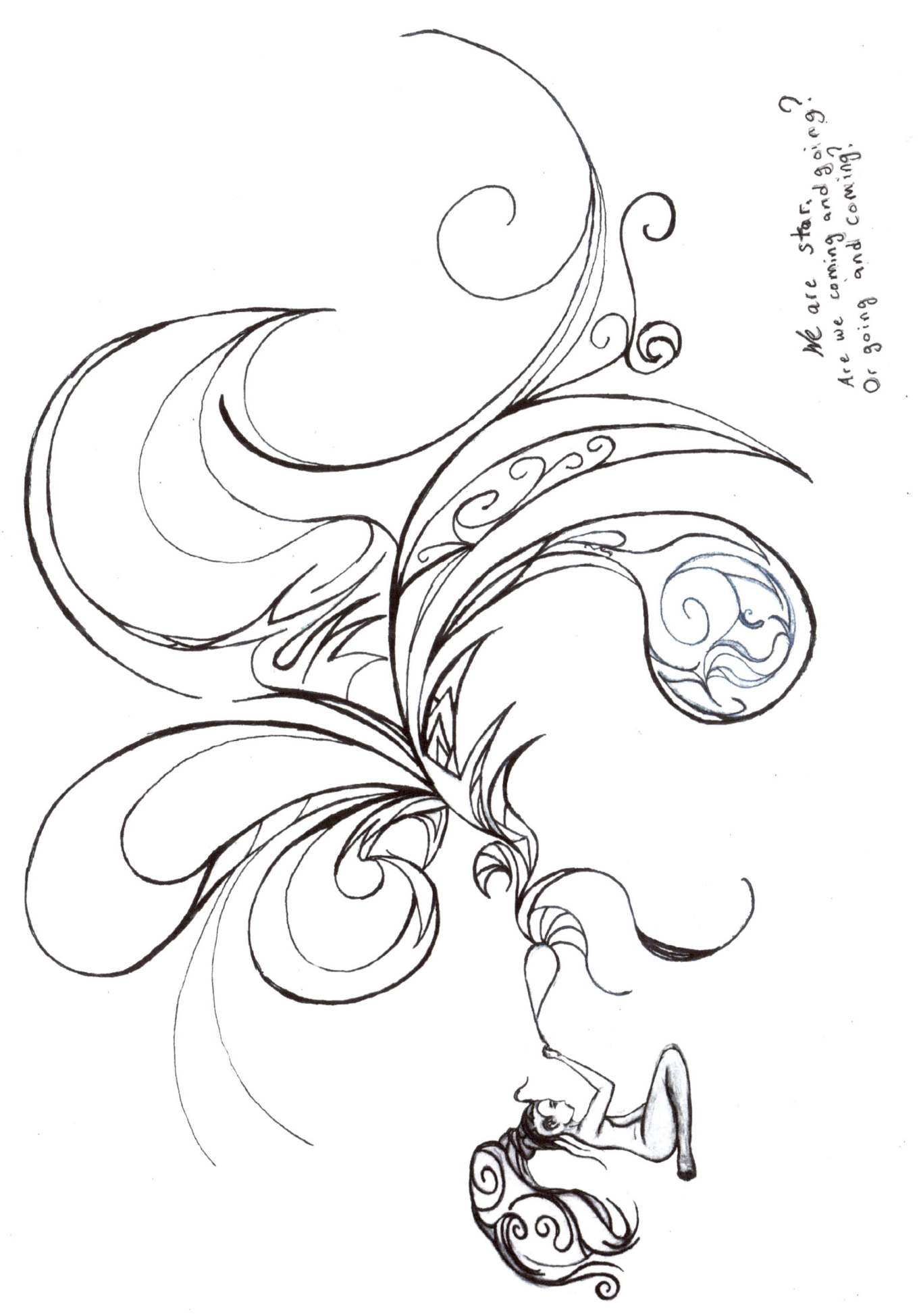

We are star.
Are we coming and going?
Or going and coming.

1/12/2016

A day prior to my birthday
I think I may become 29 years of age,
before which, I've experienced
vortex after vortex... I'm drifting in one momentarily
Really sure I'm drifting.

Somehow though, I've accomplished and seen most
of what I only believed were dreams.
Sadly the map to this very location is
apparently lost.

Aborting.. As usual.

Somehow discovering myself trying to
be in an adventure that only
I possess a Perspective to.

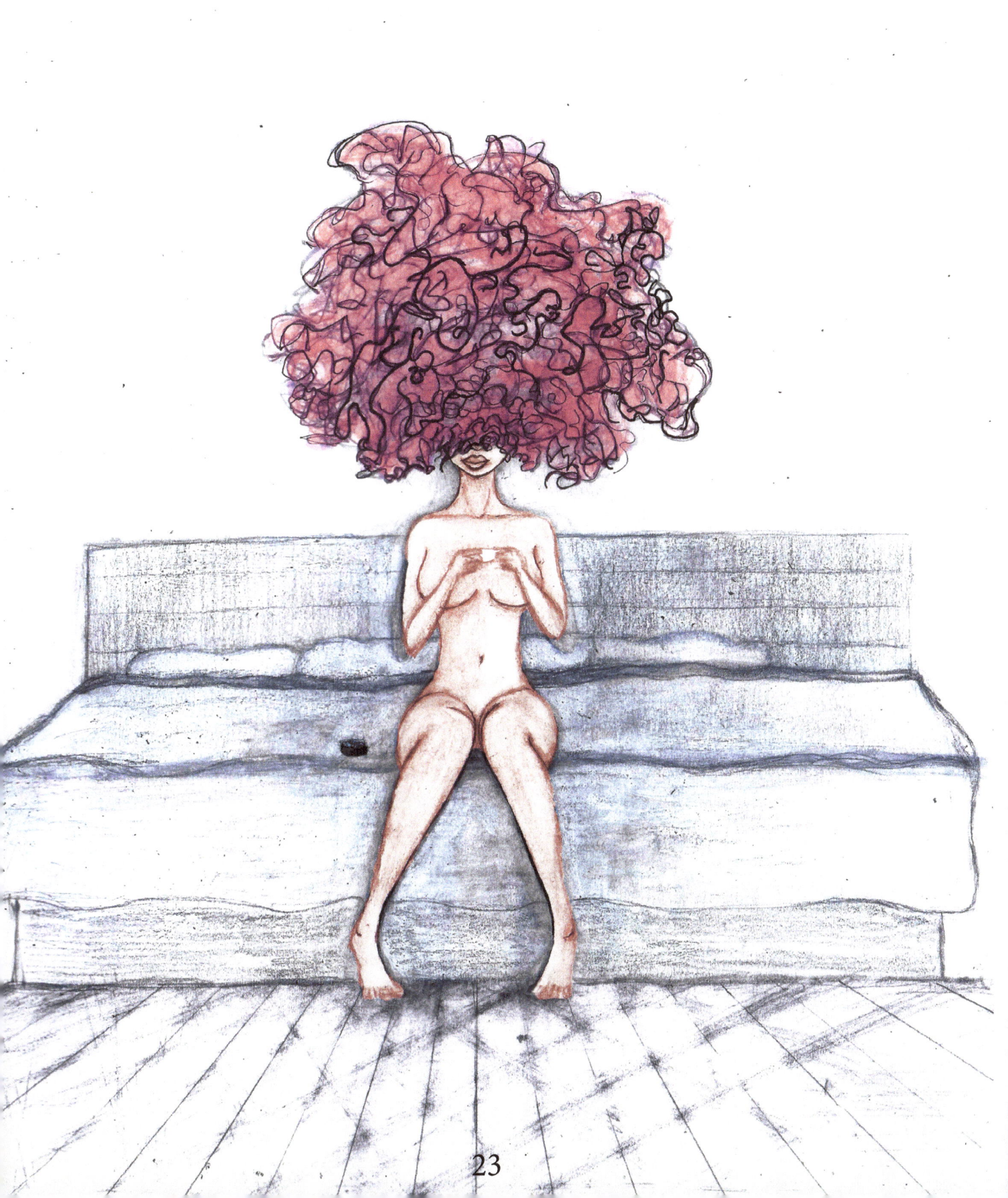

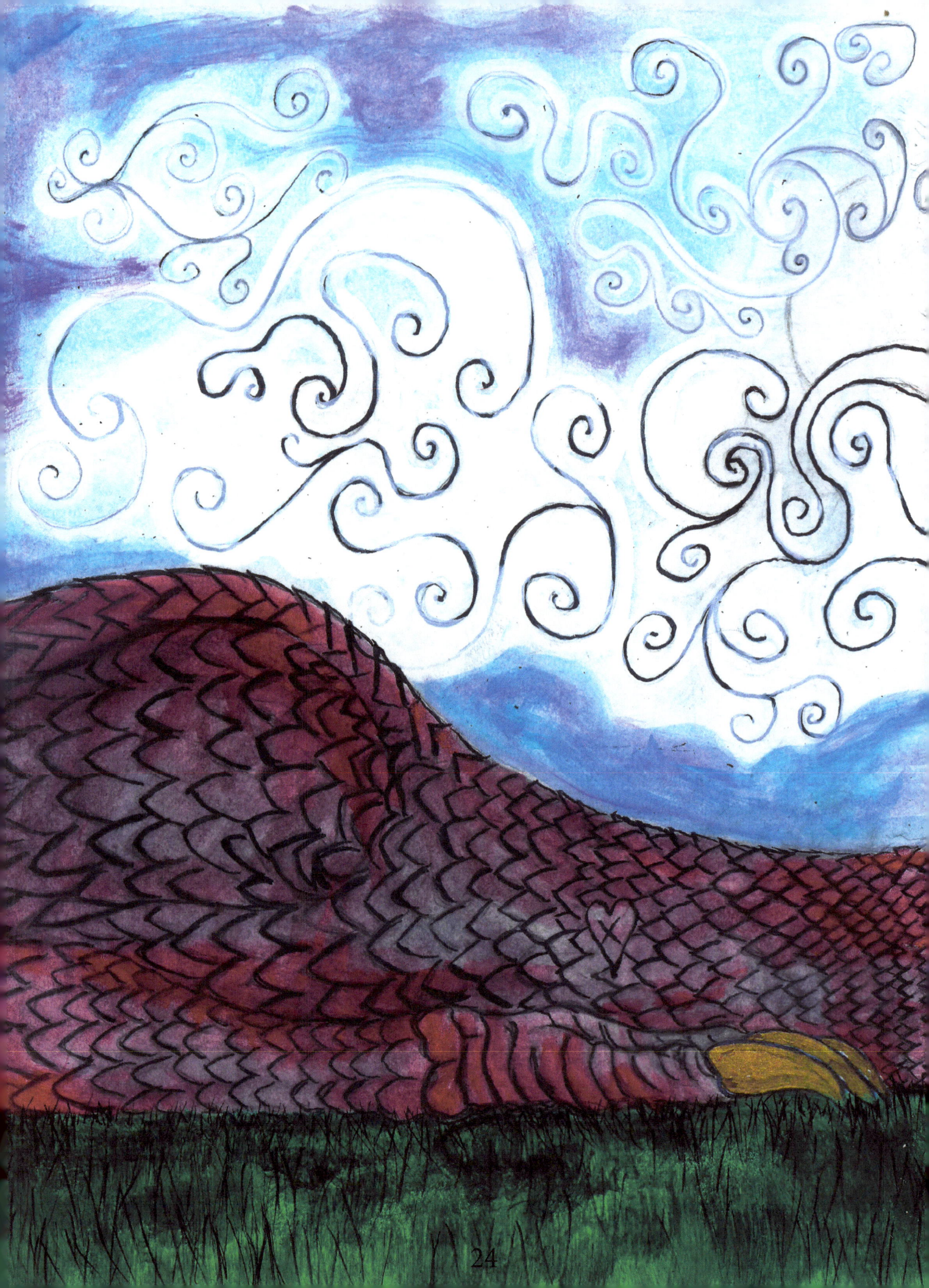

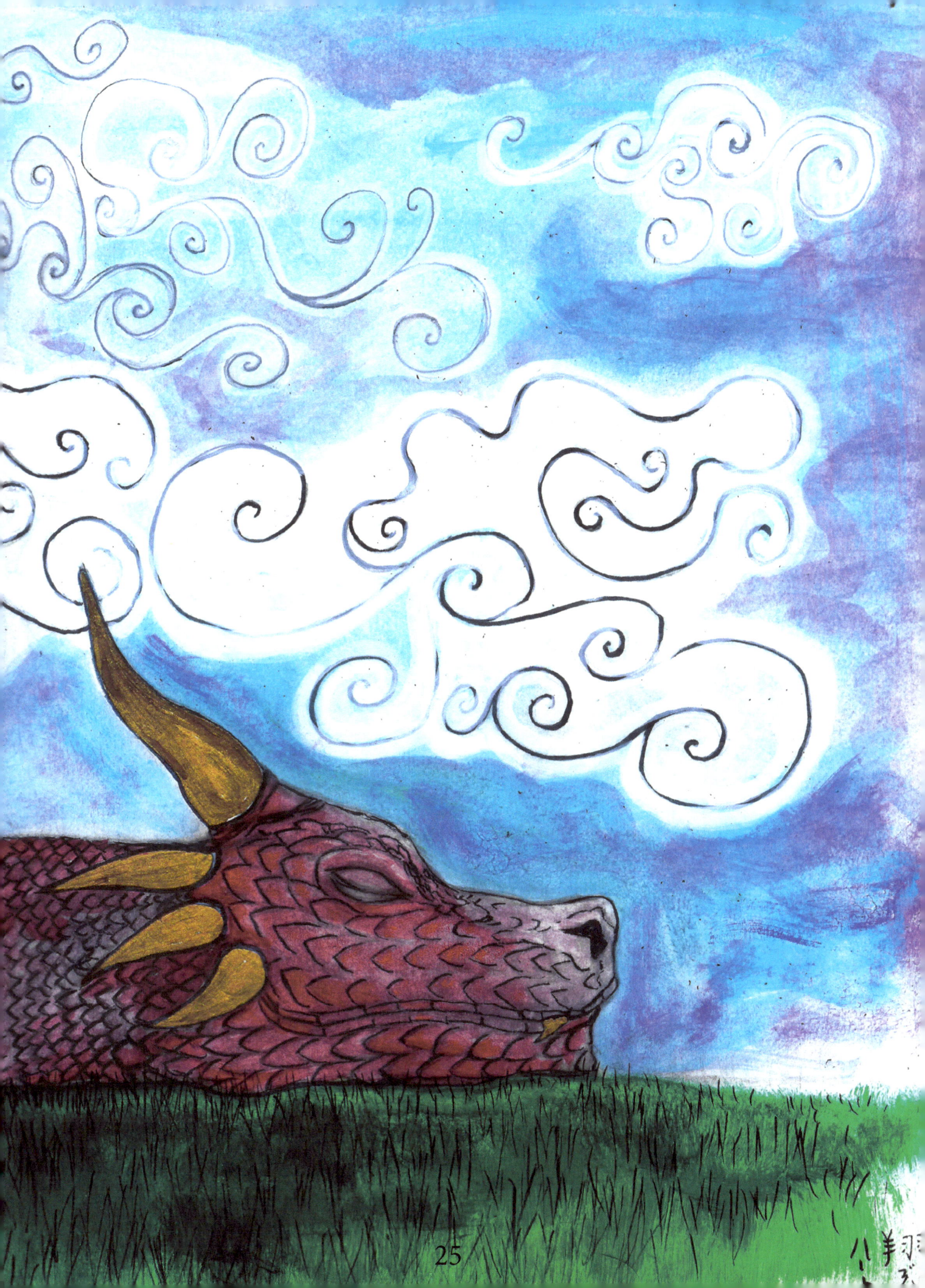

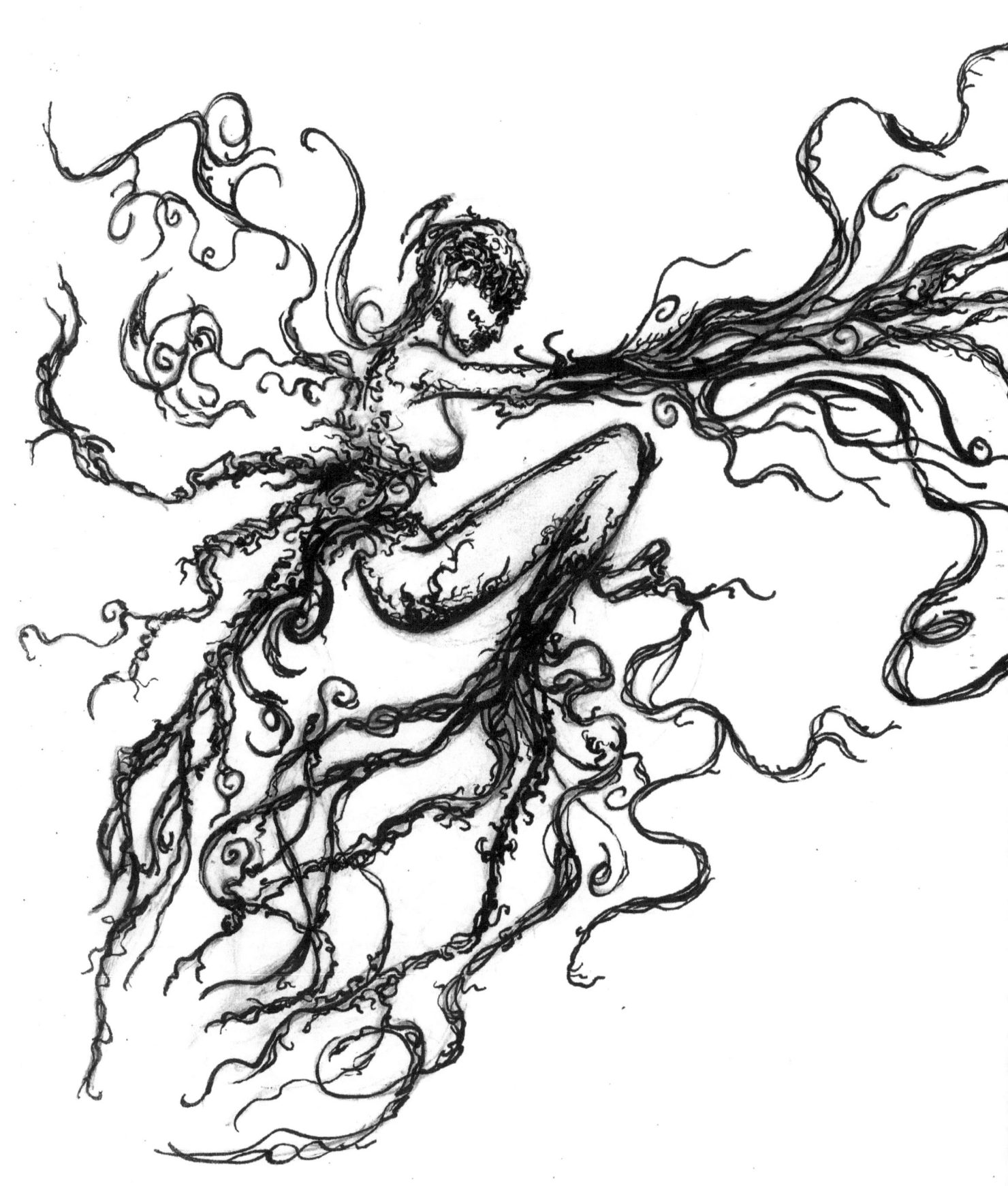

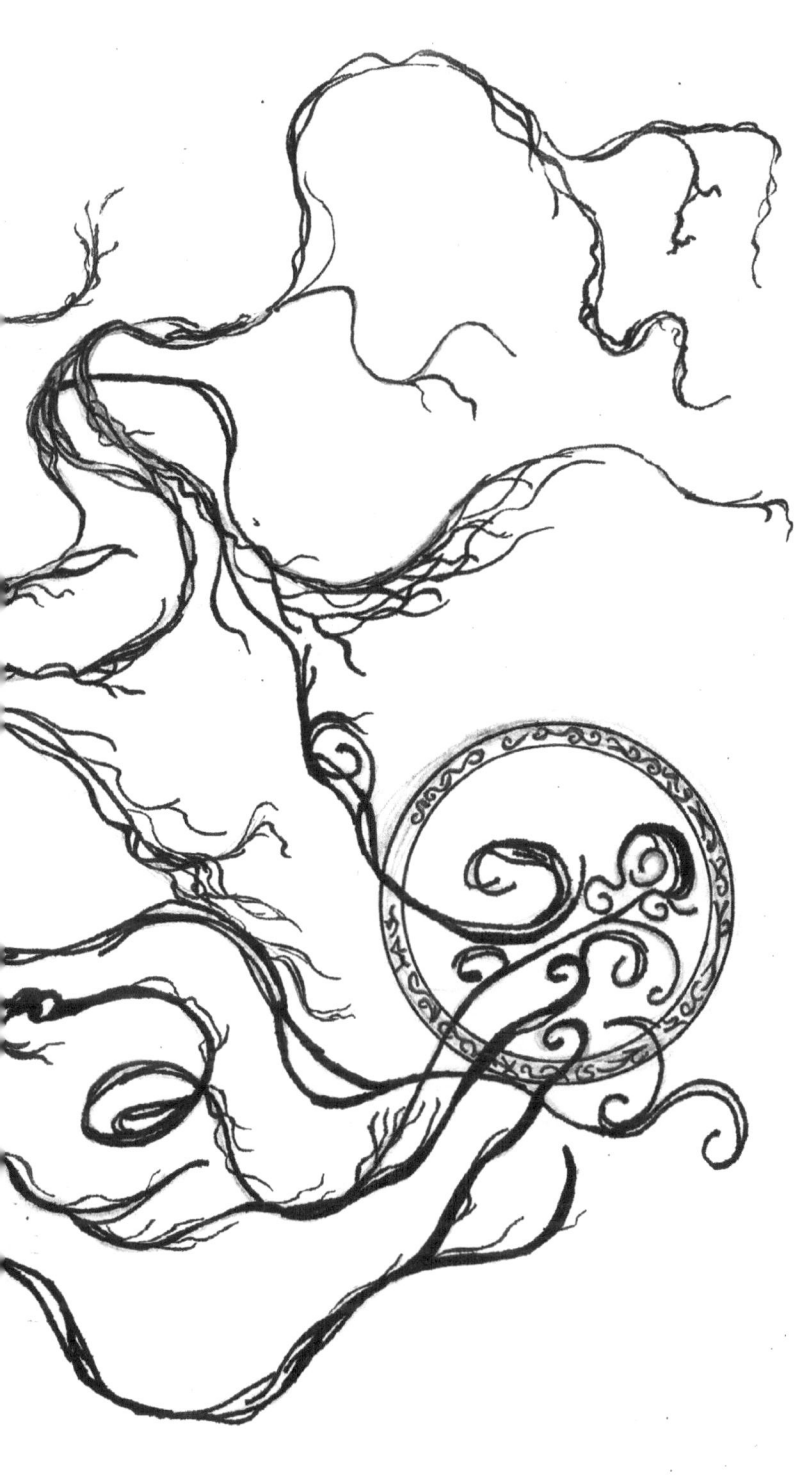

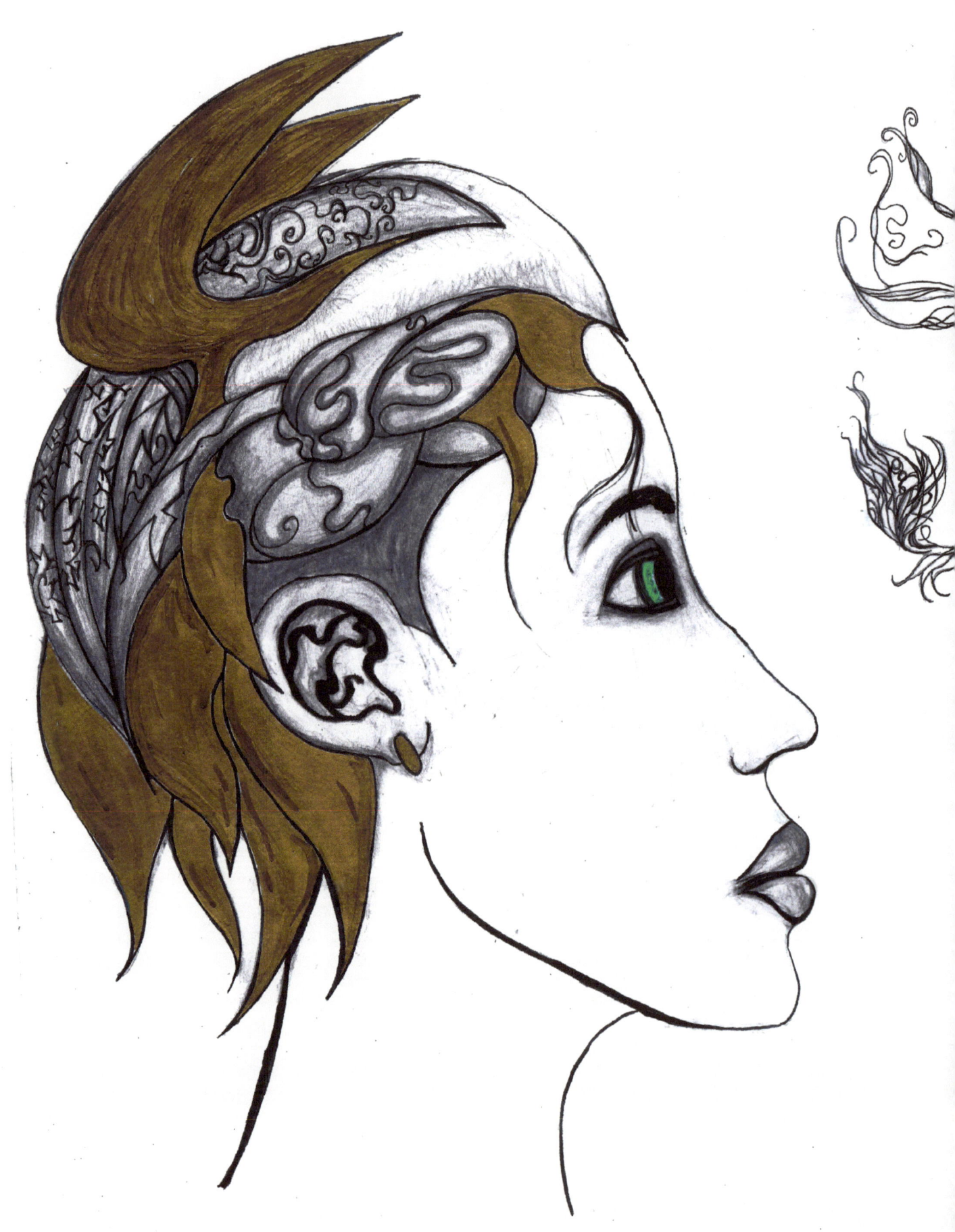

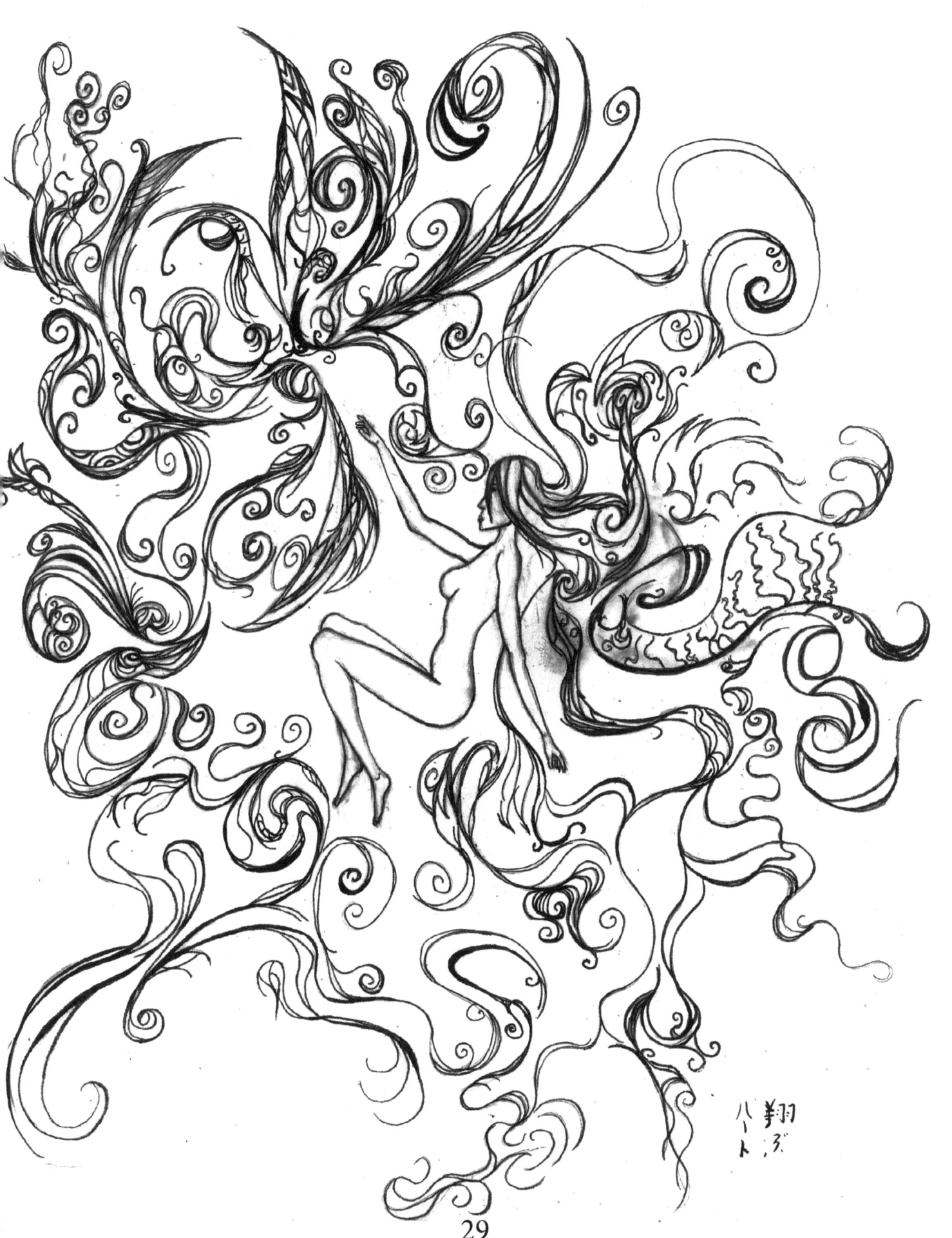

29

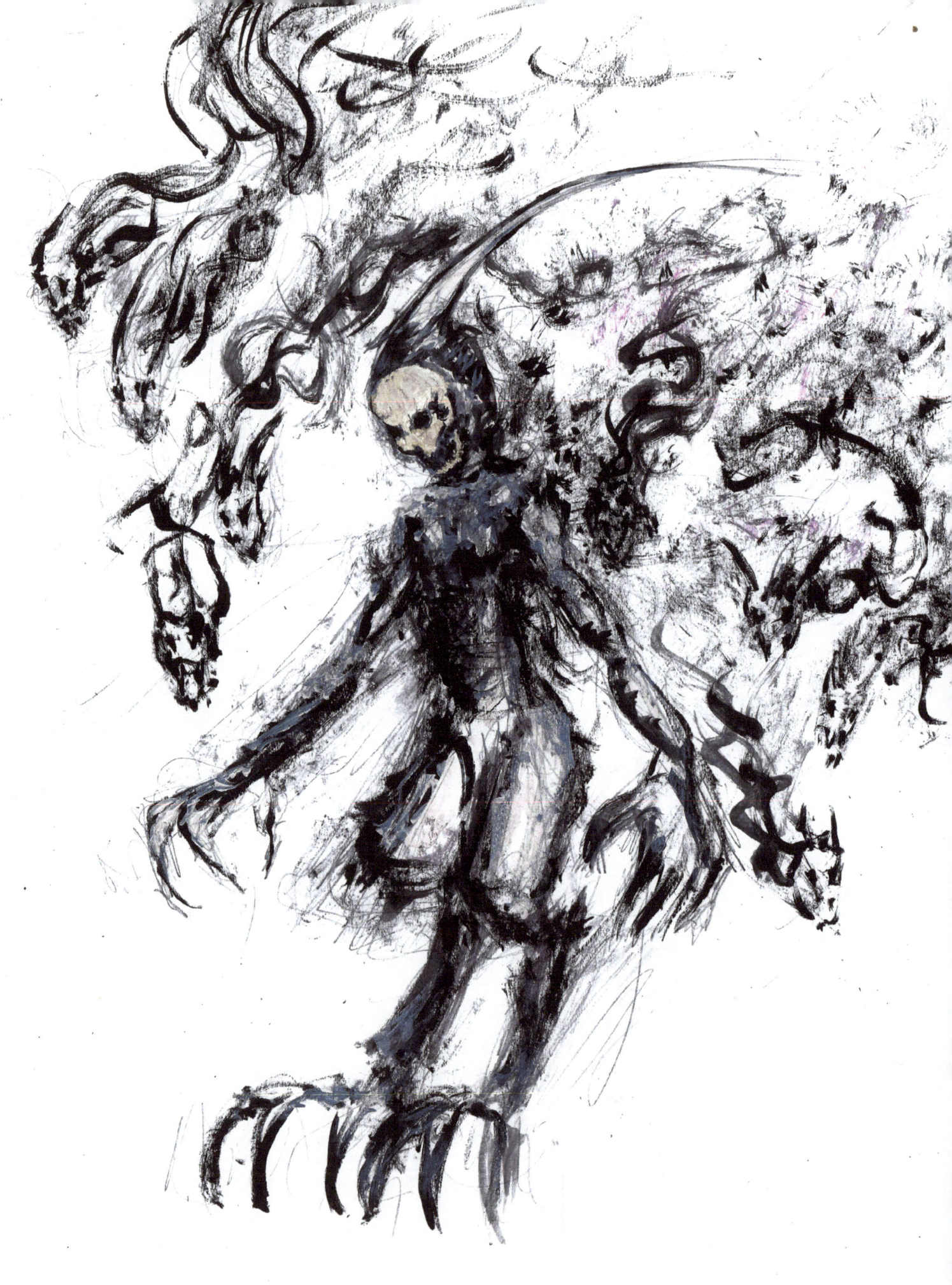

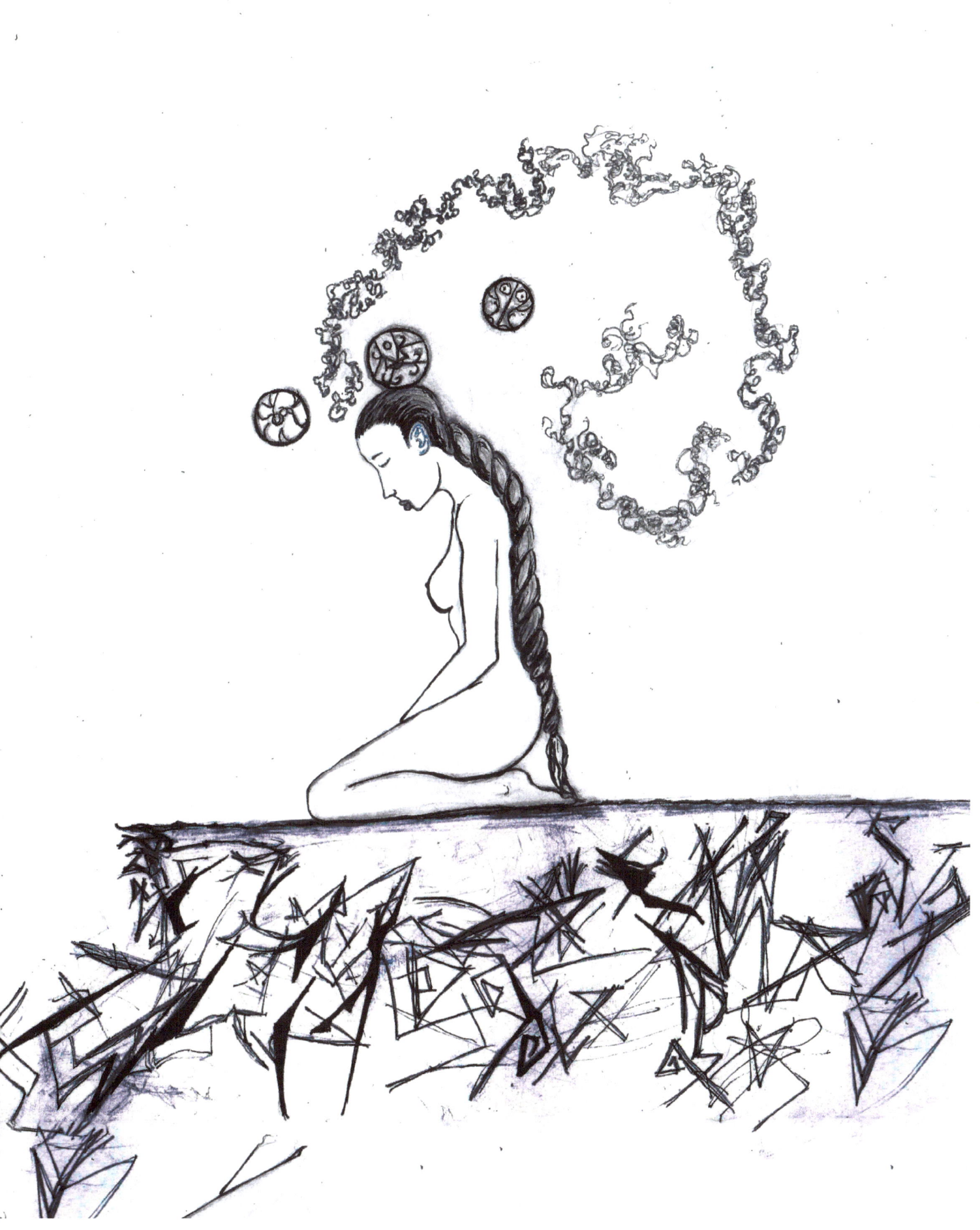

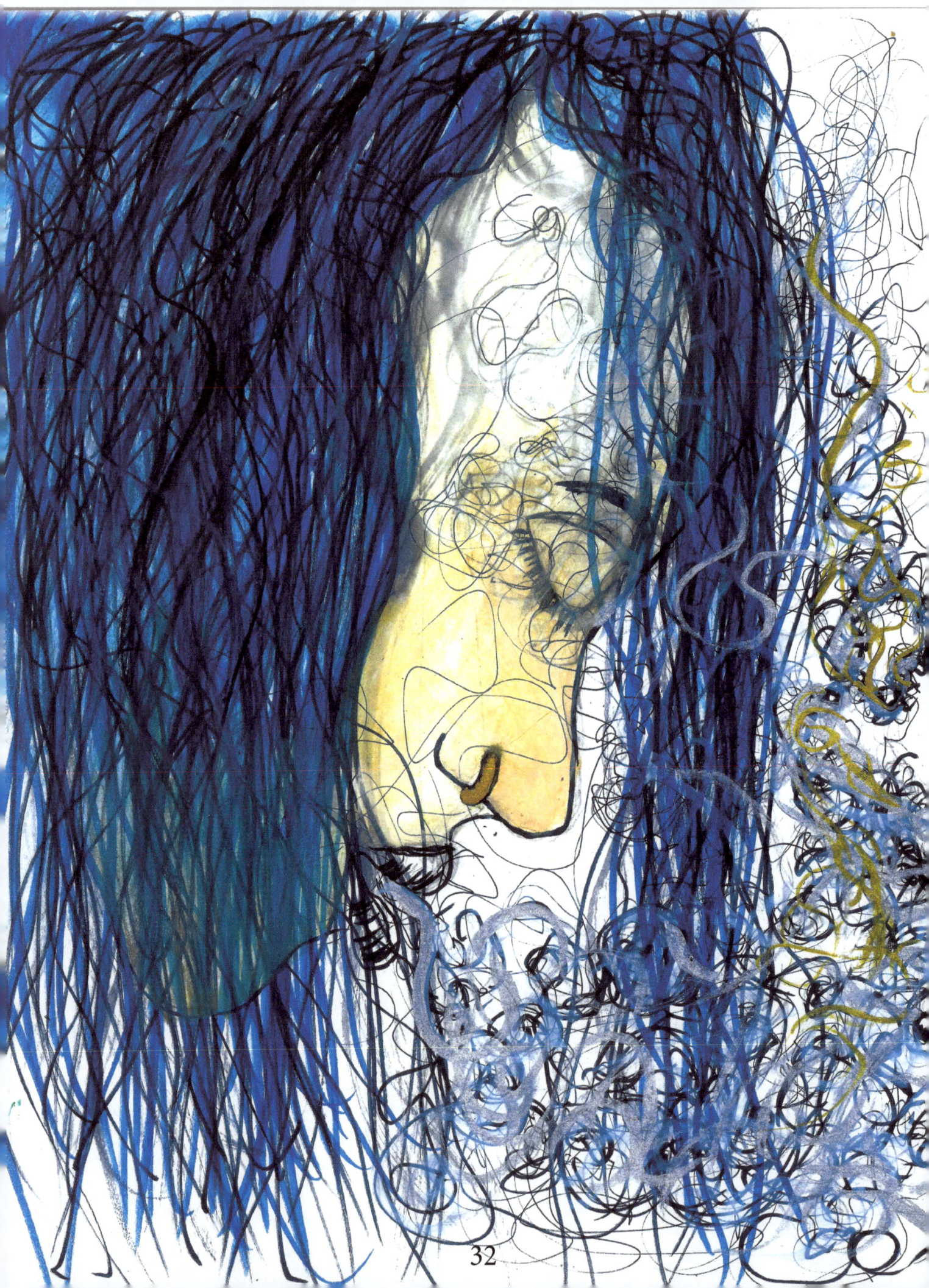

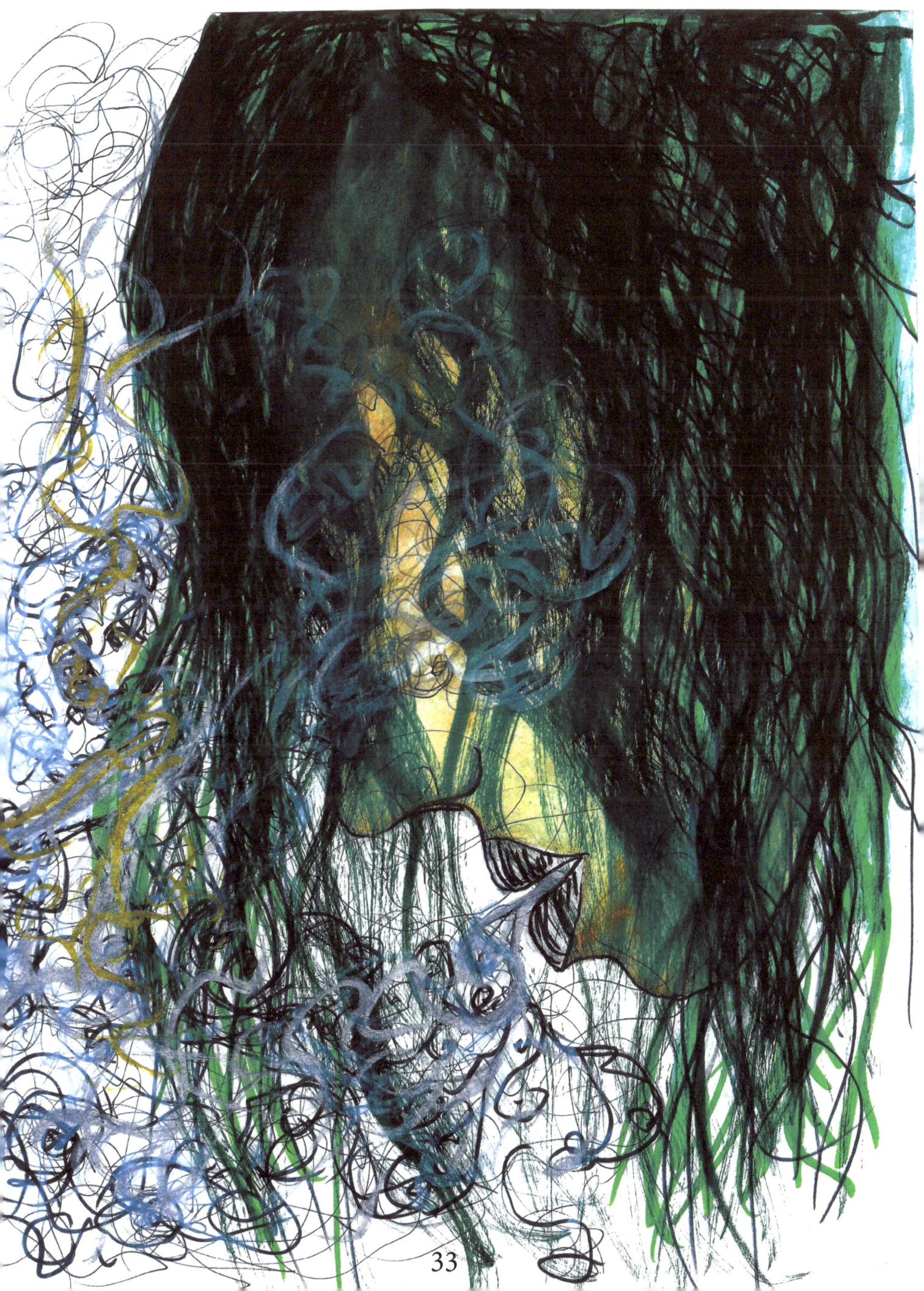

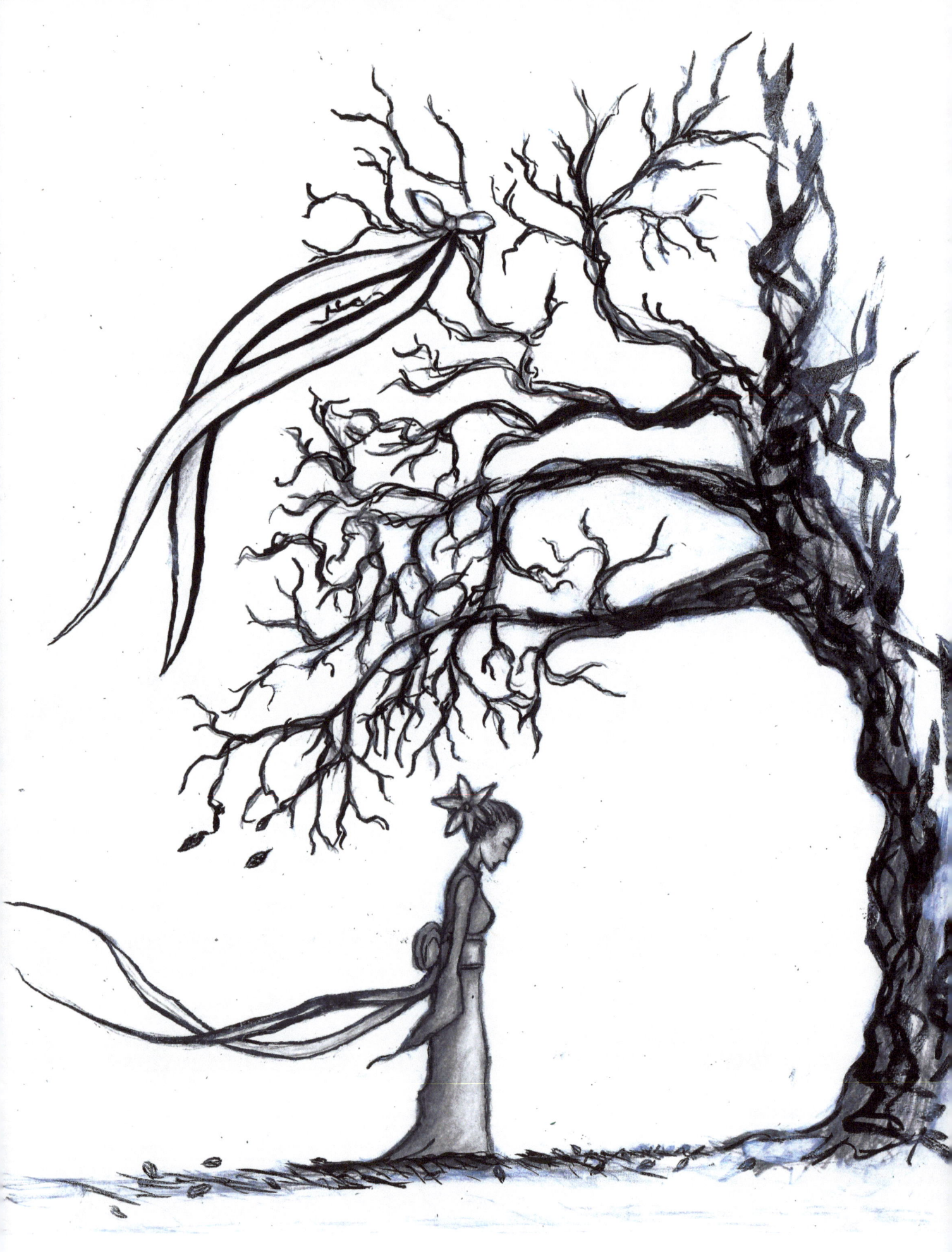

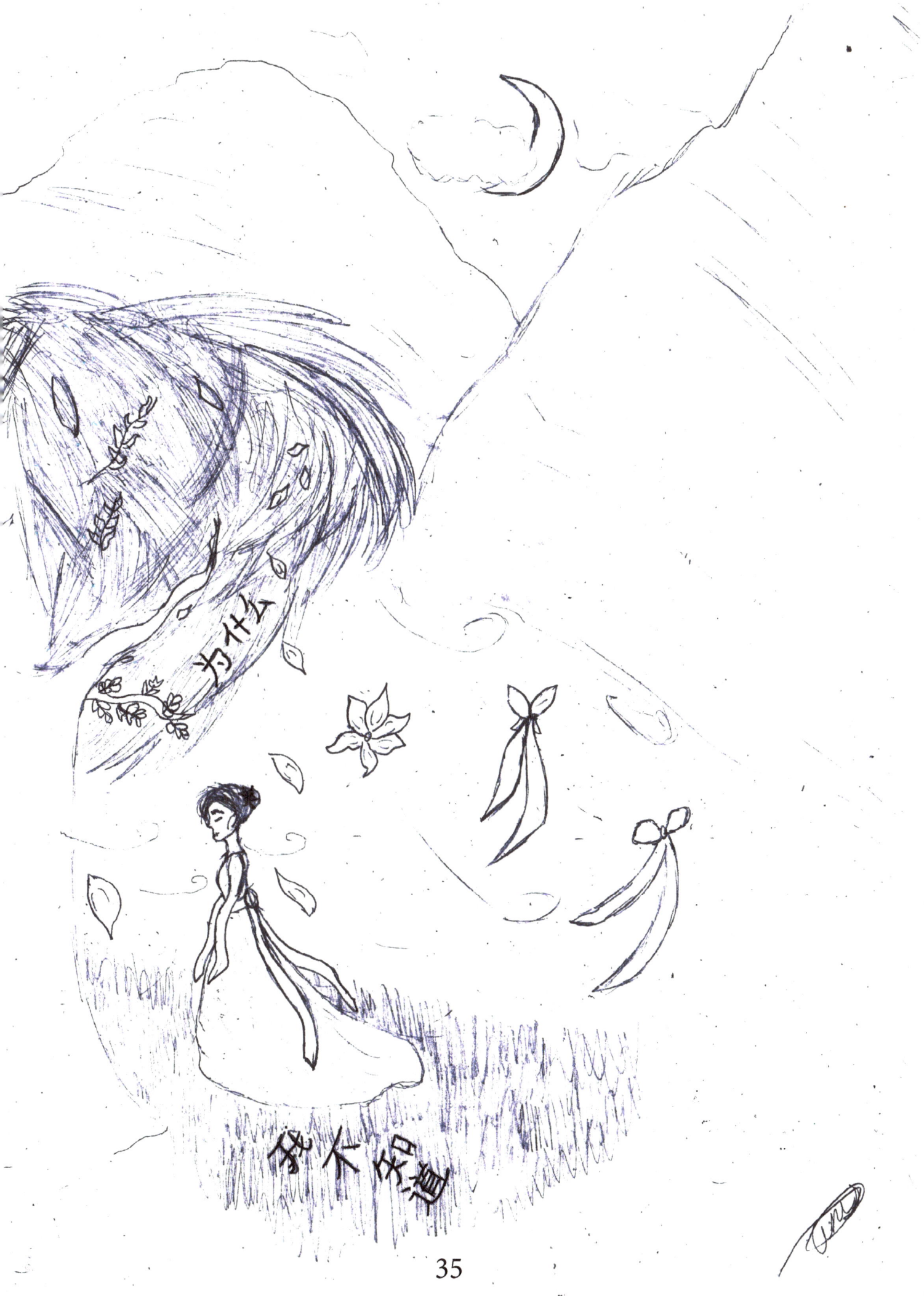

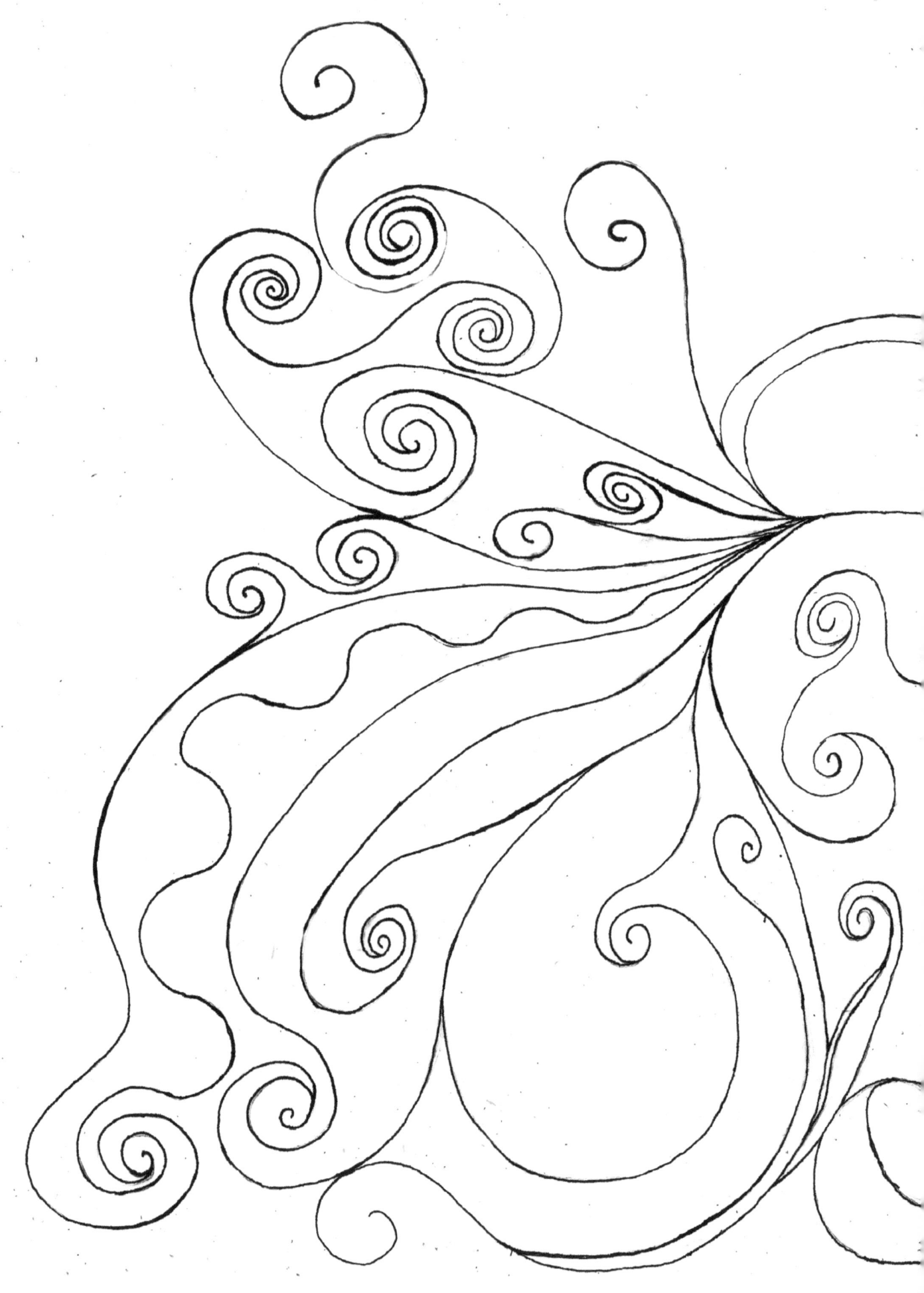

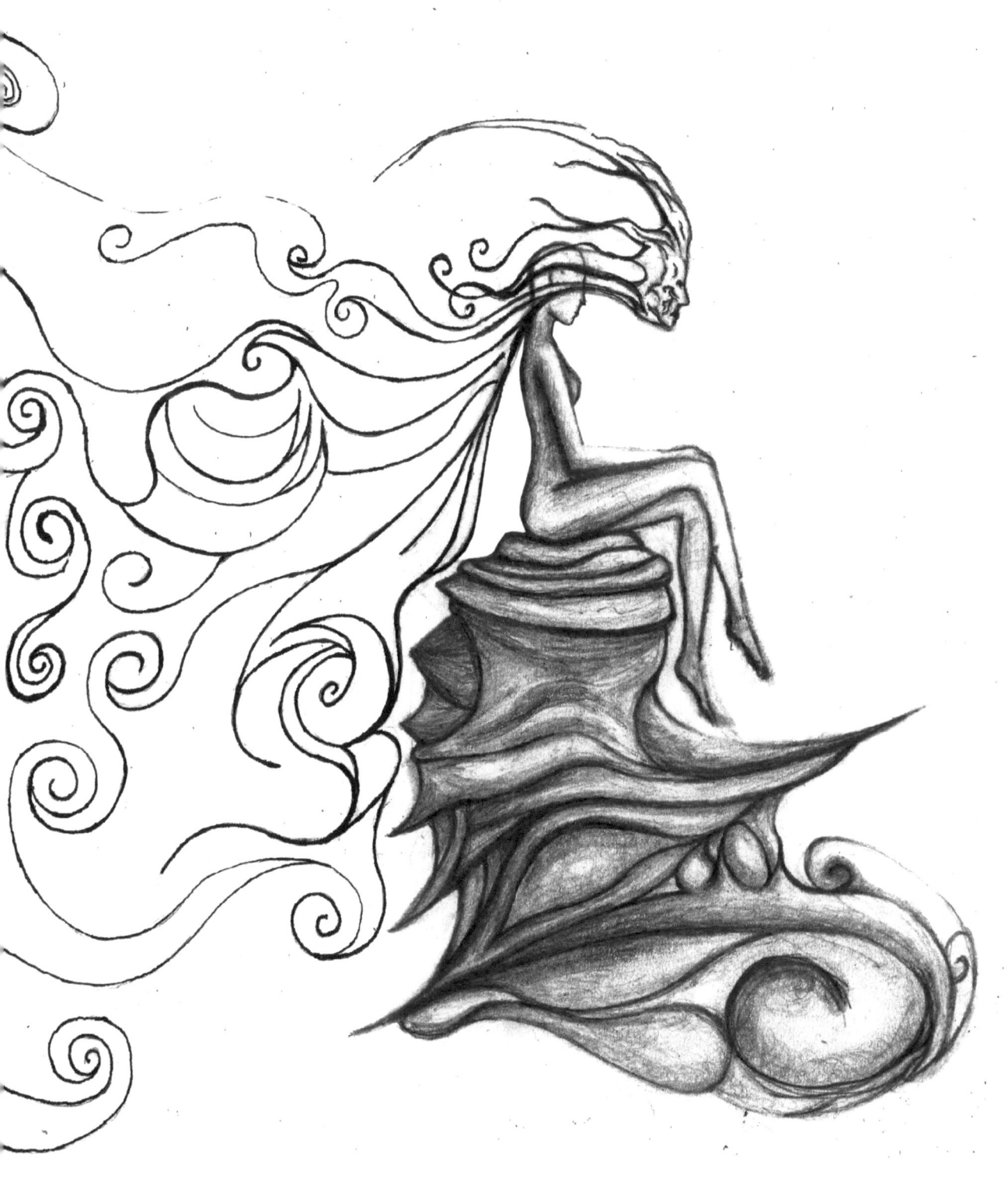

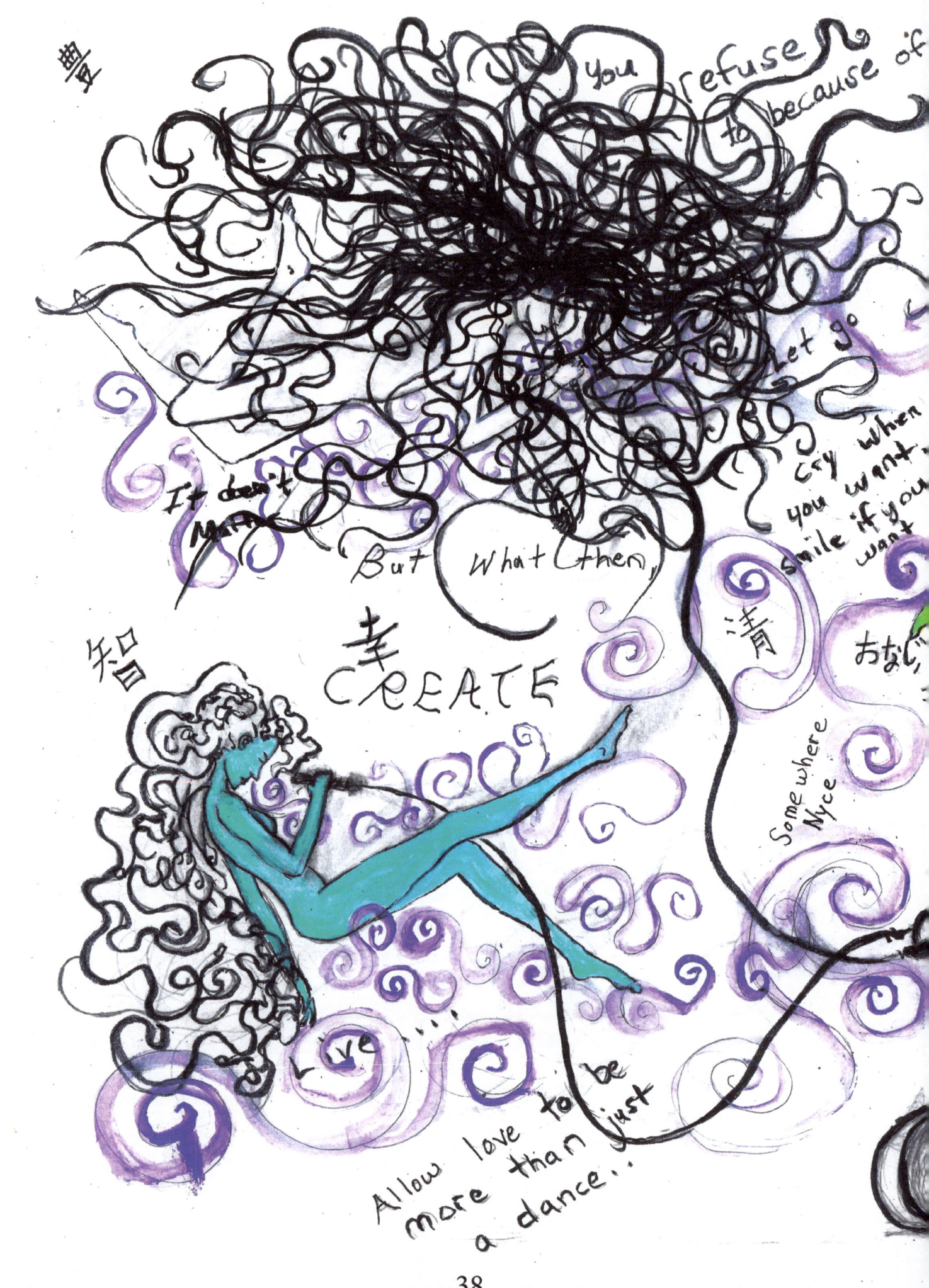

豊

you refuse to because of

Let go

cry when you want. smile if you want

It don't matter

But What then

清

おなじ

智

幸
CREATE

Somewhere Nyce

Allow love to be more than just a dance...

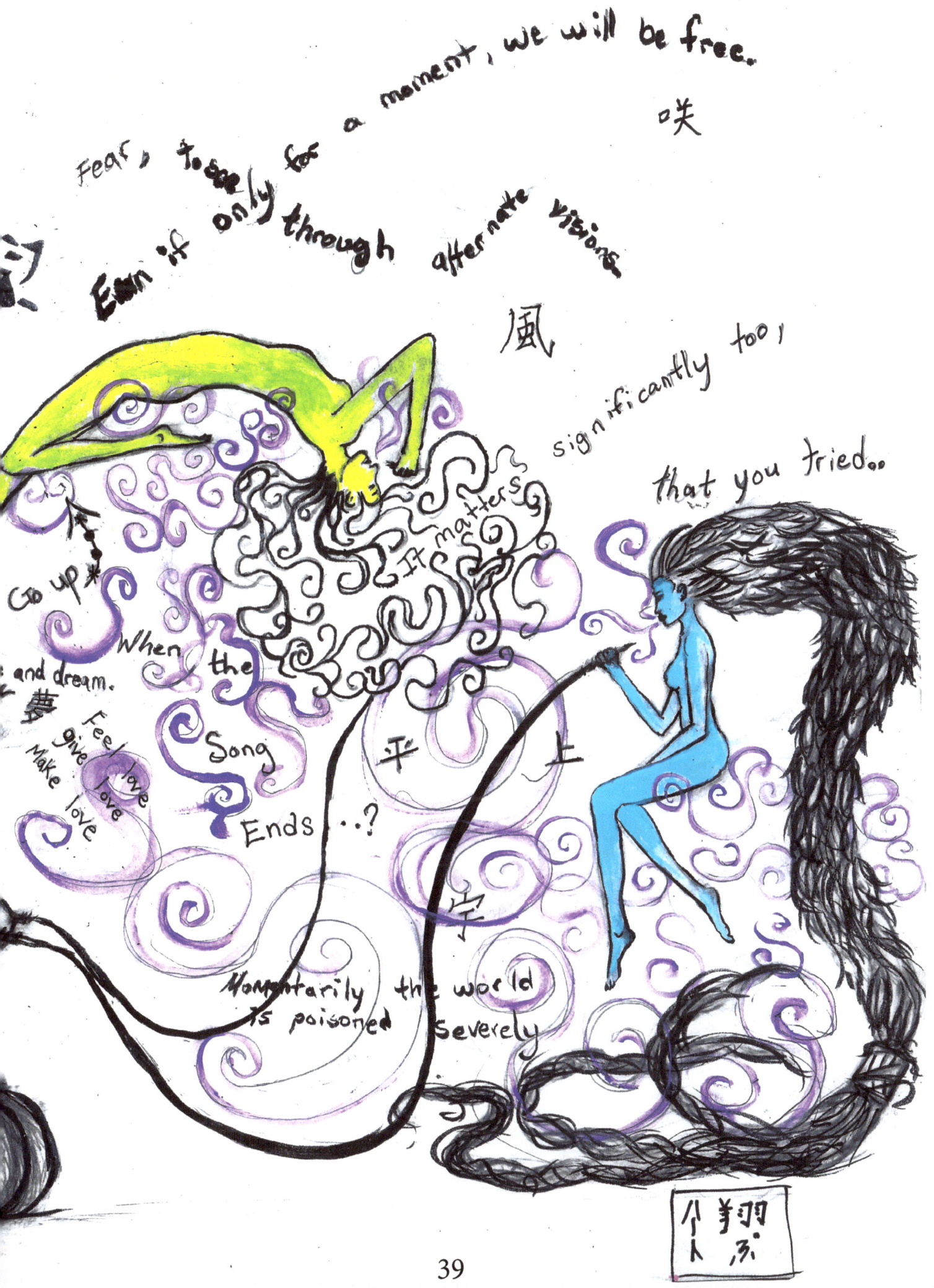

Fear, to see only for a moment, we will be free.

咲

Even if only through alternate visions

風

significantly too,

that you tried..

Go up

and dream.

When the

Song

Ends ...?

Feel love
give love
Make love

It matters

平

上

空

Momentarily the world
is poisoned severely

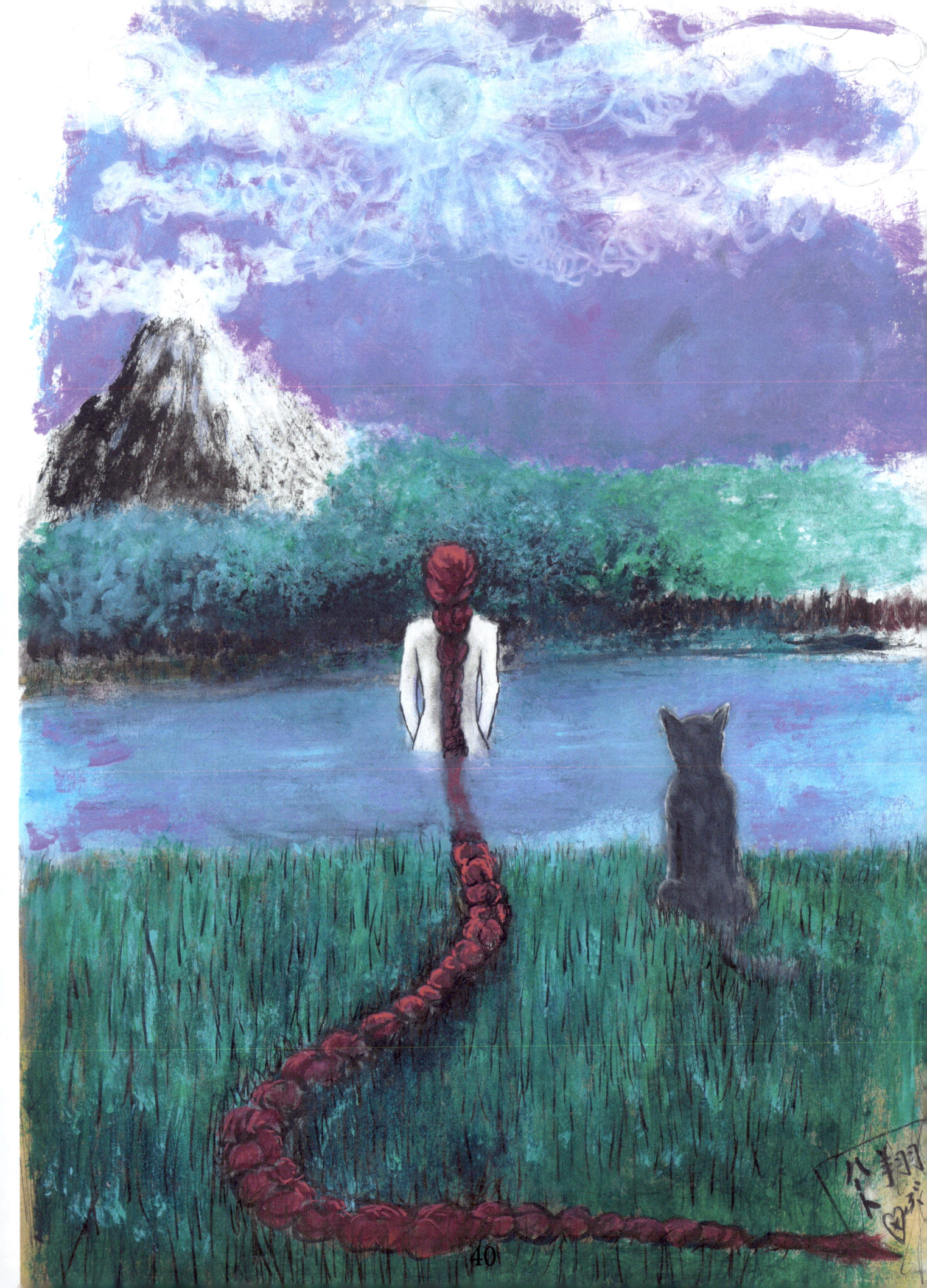

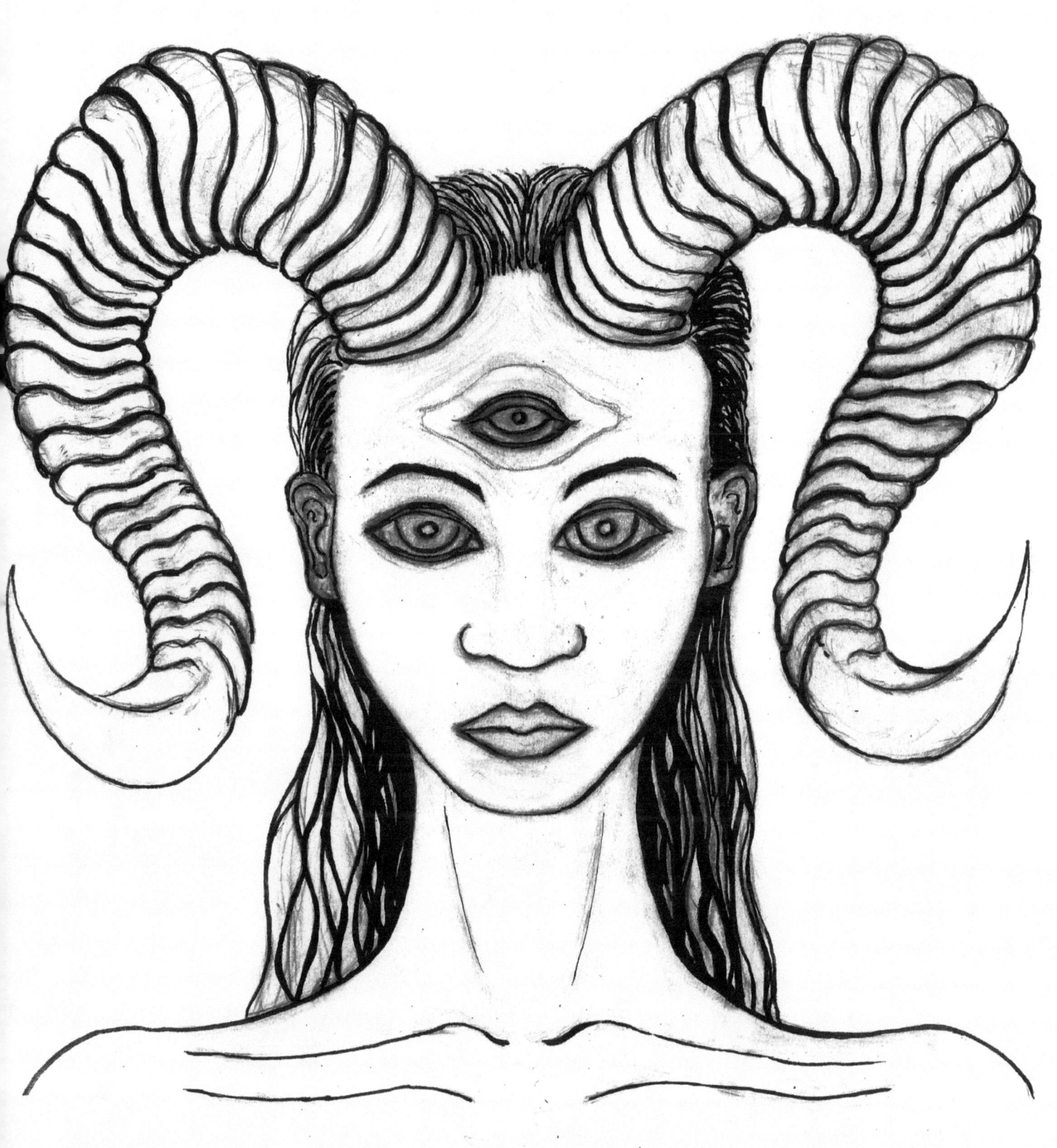

41

羽翔
ハート
ぶ゛

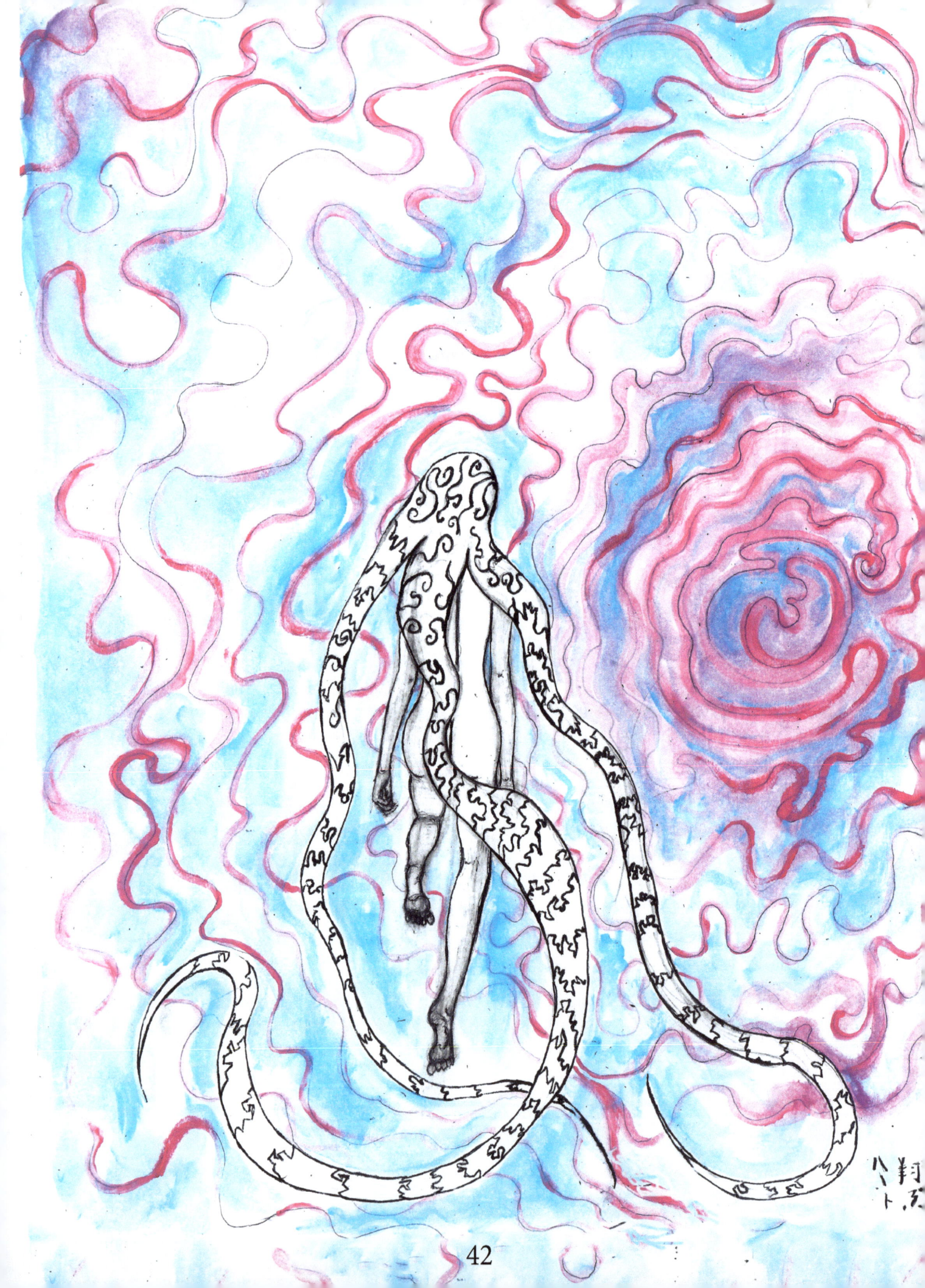

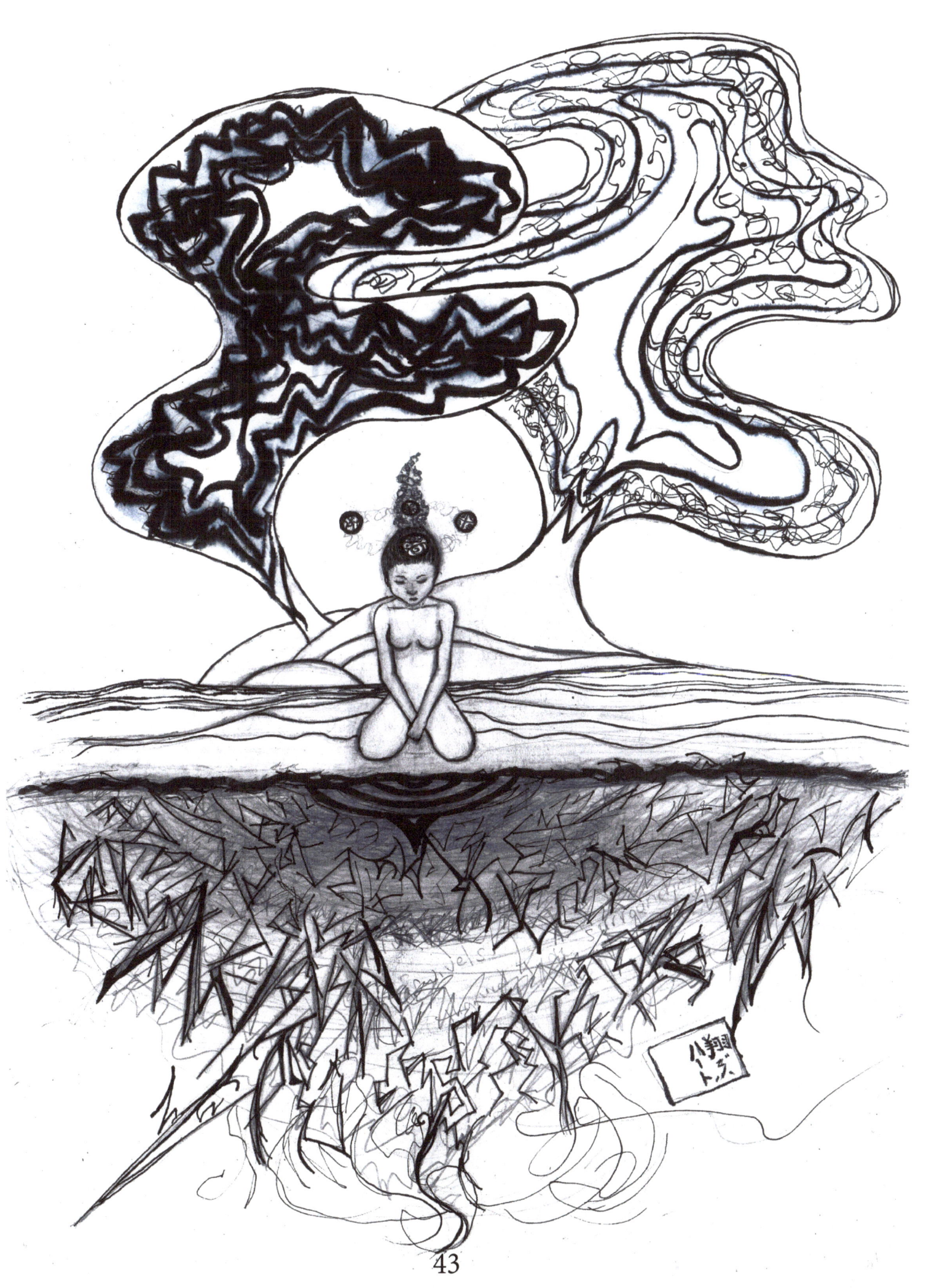

43

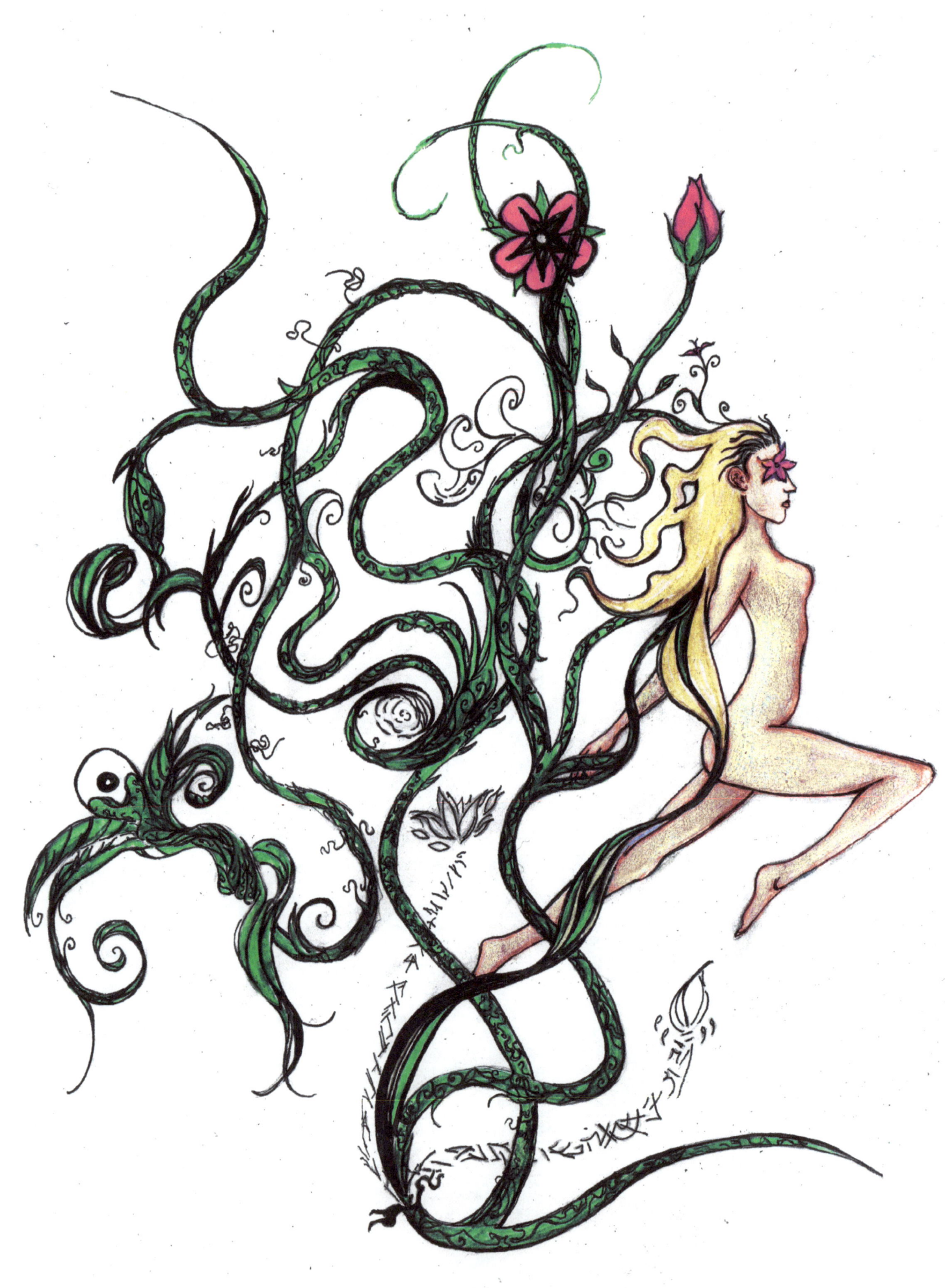

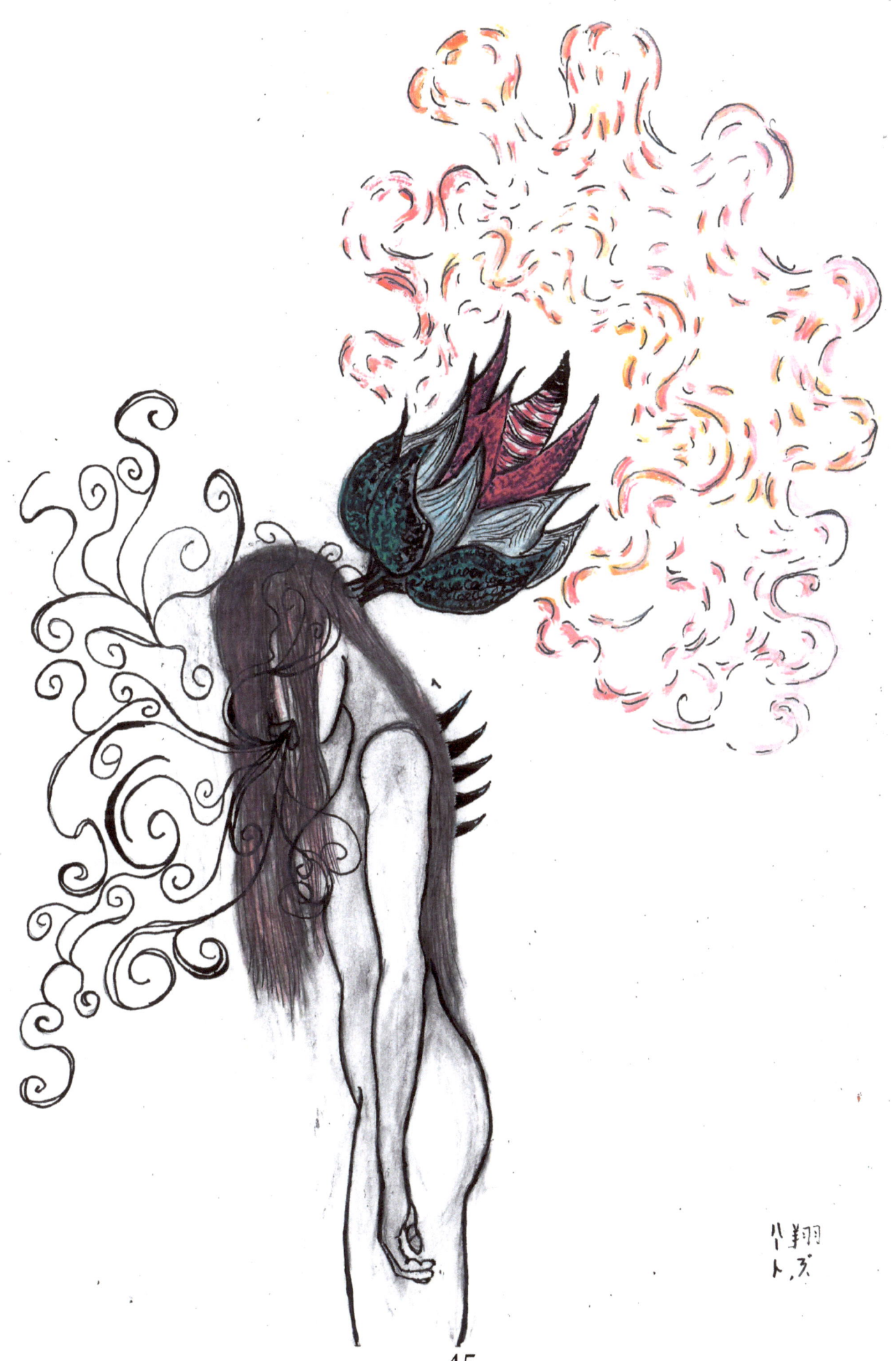

45

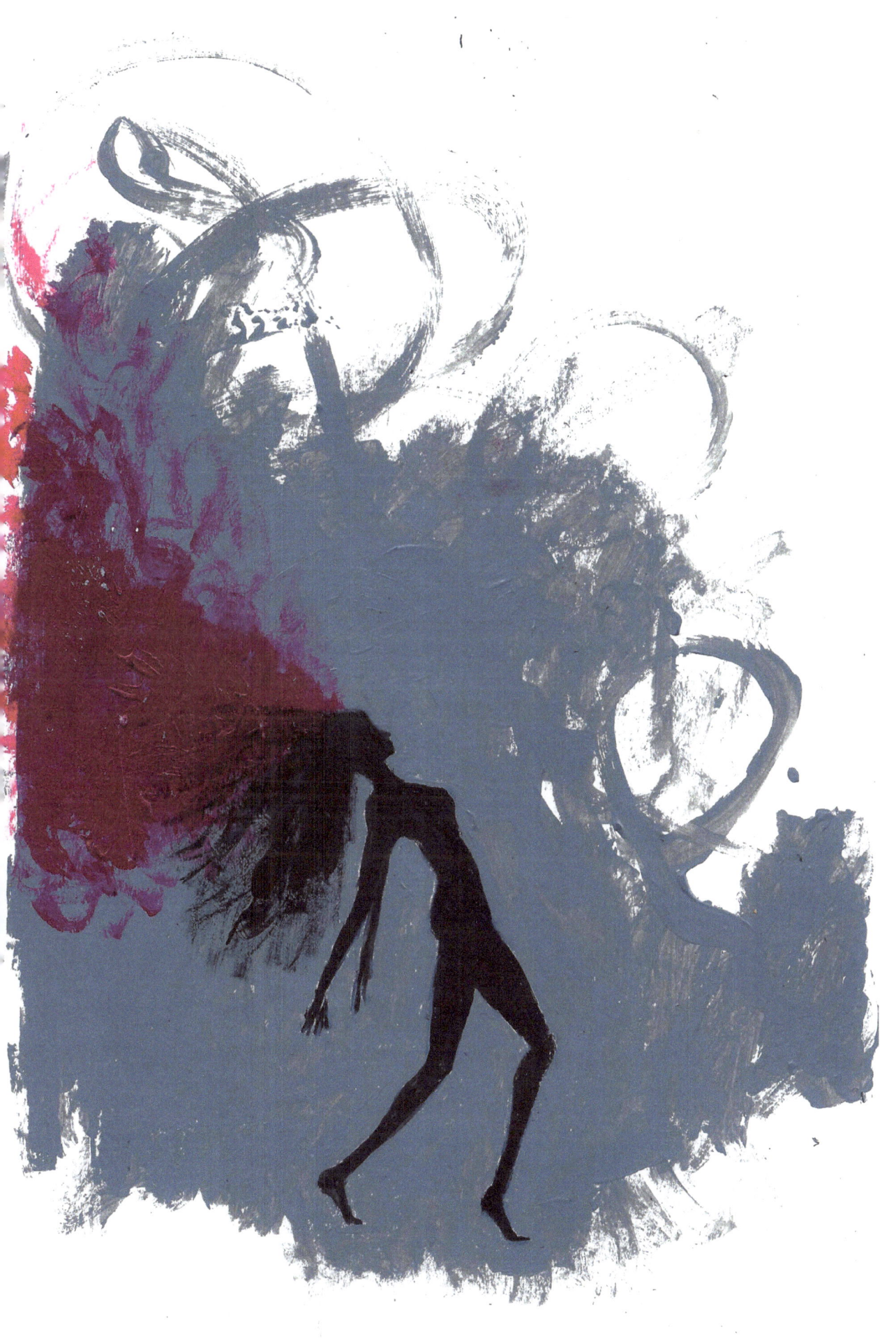

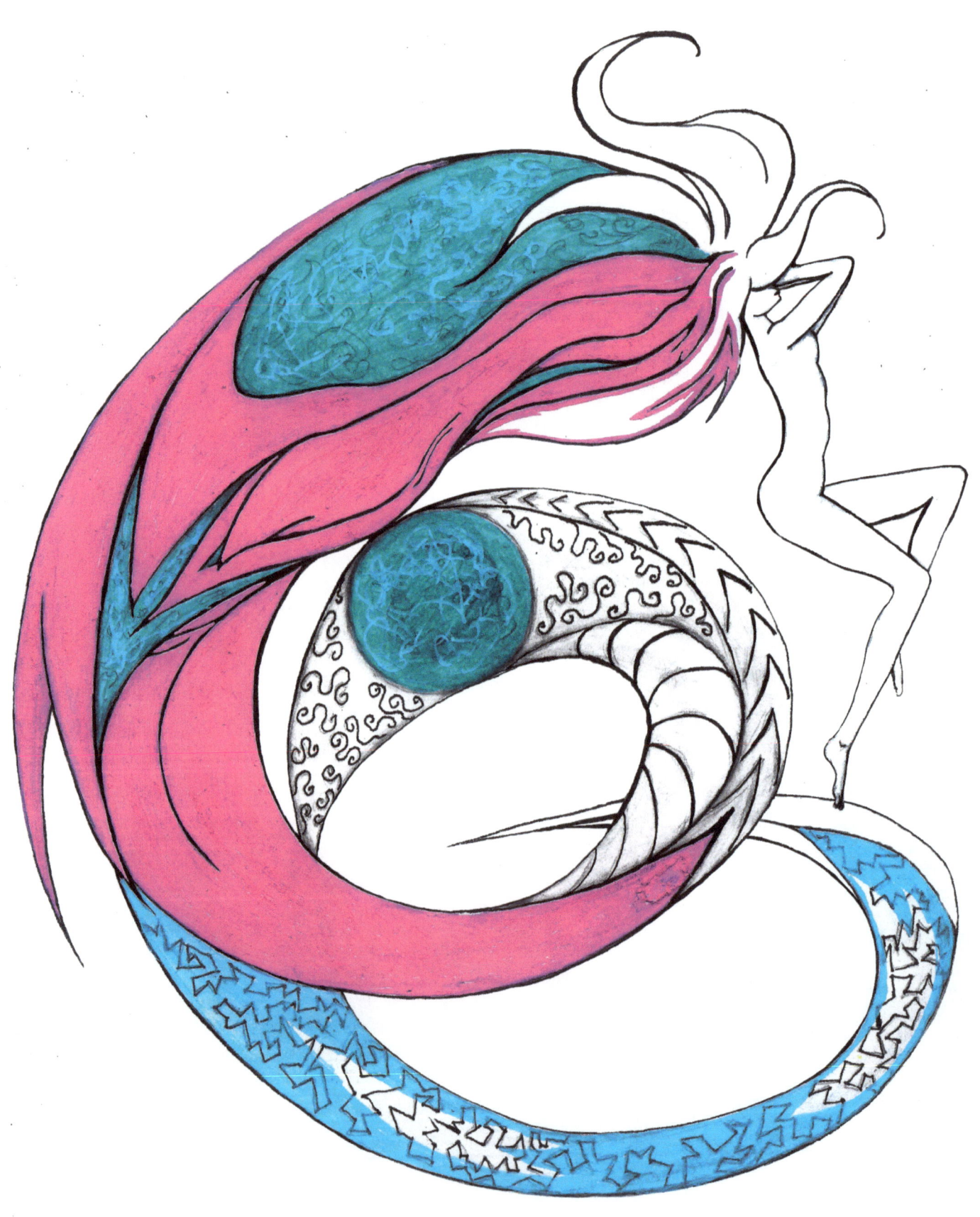

48

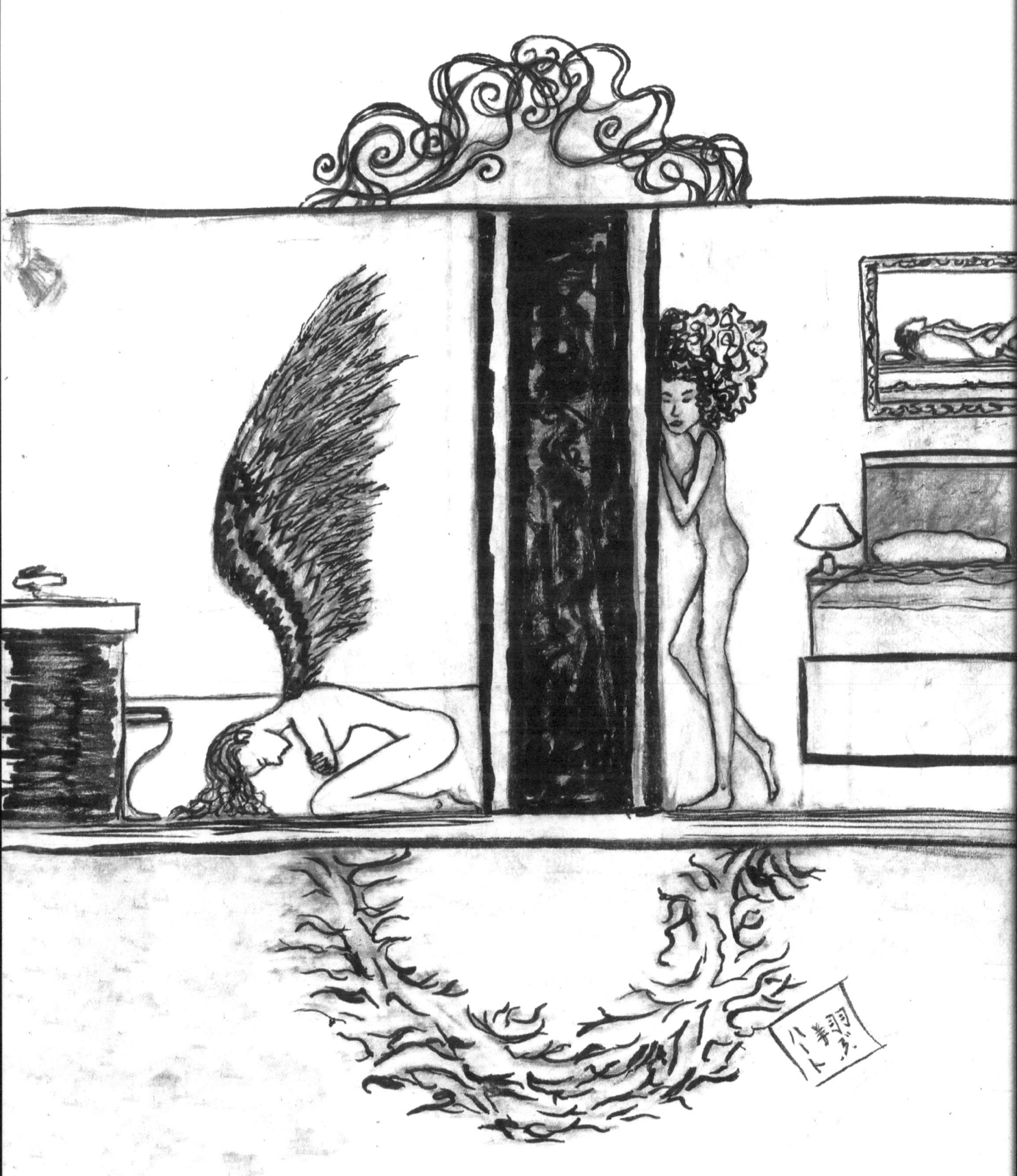

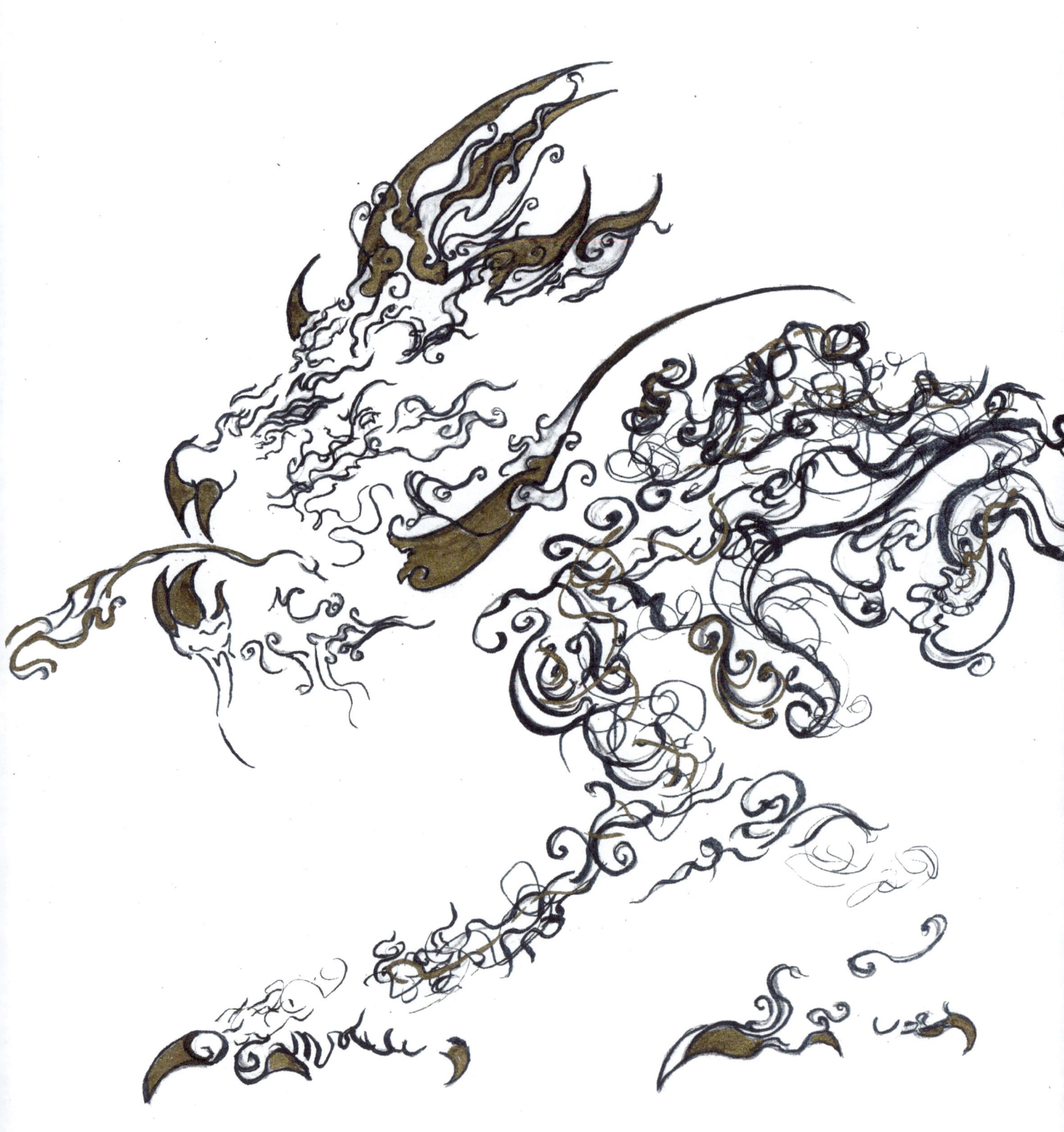

50

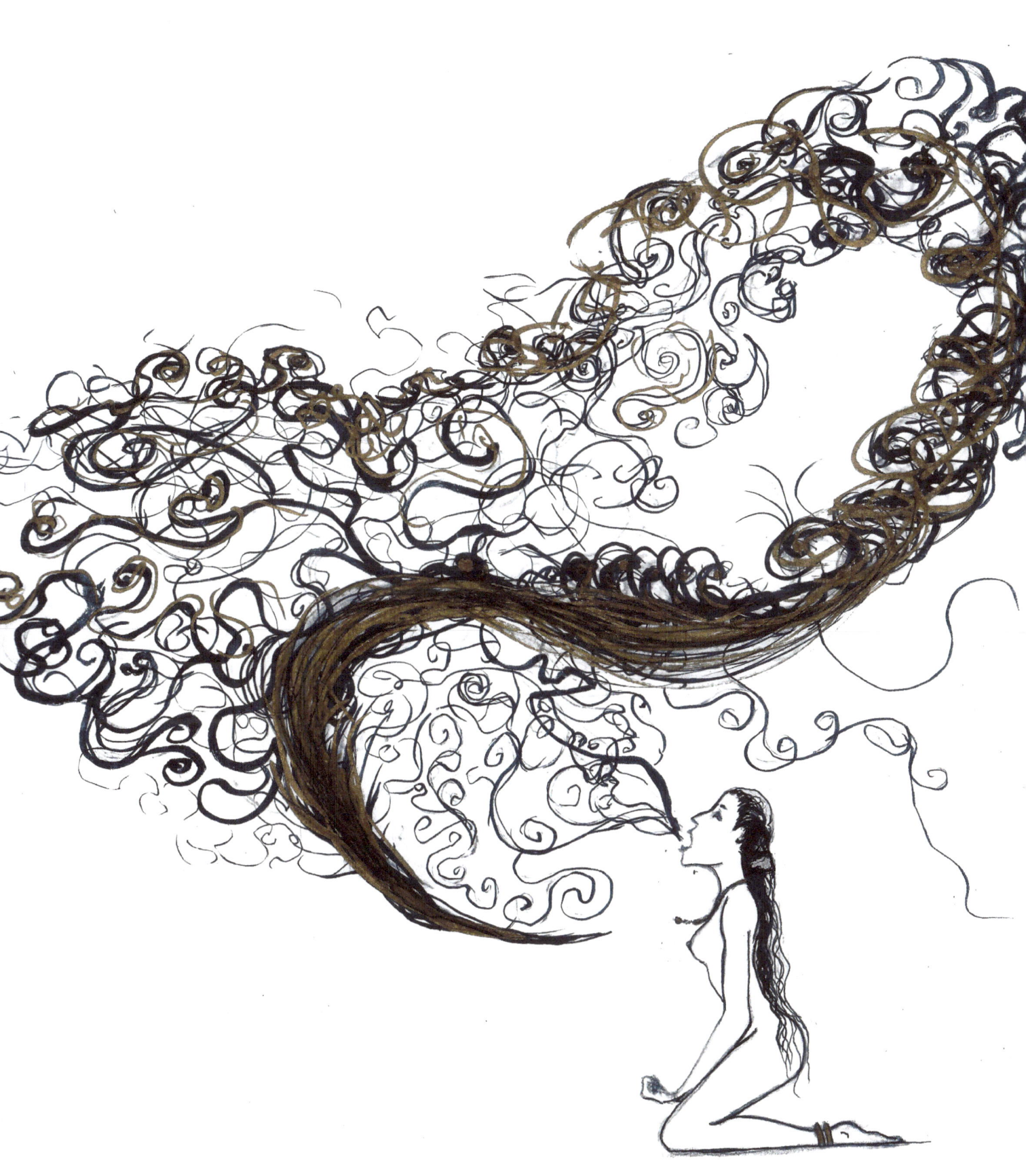

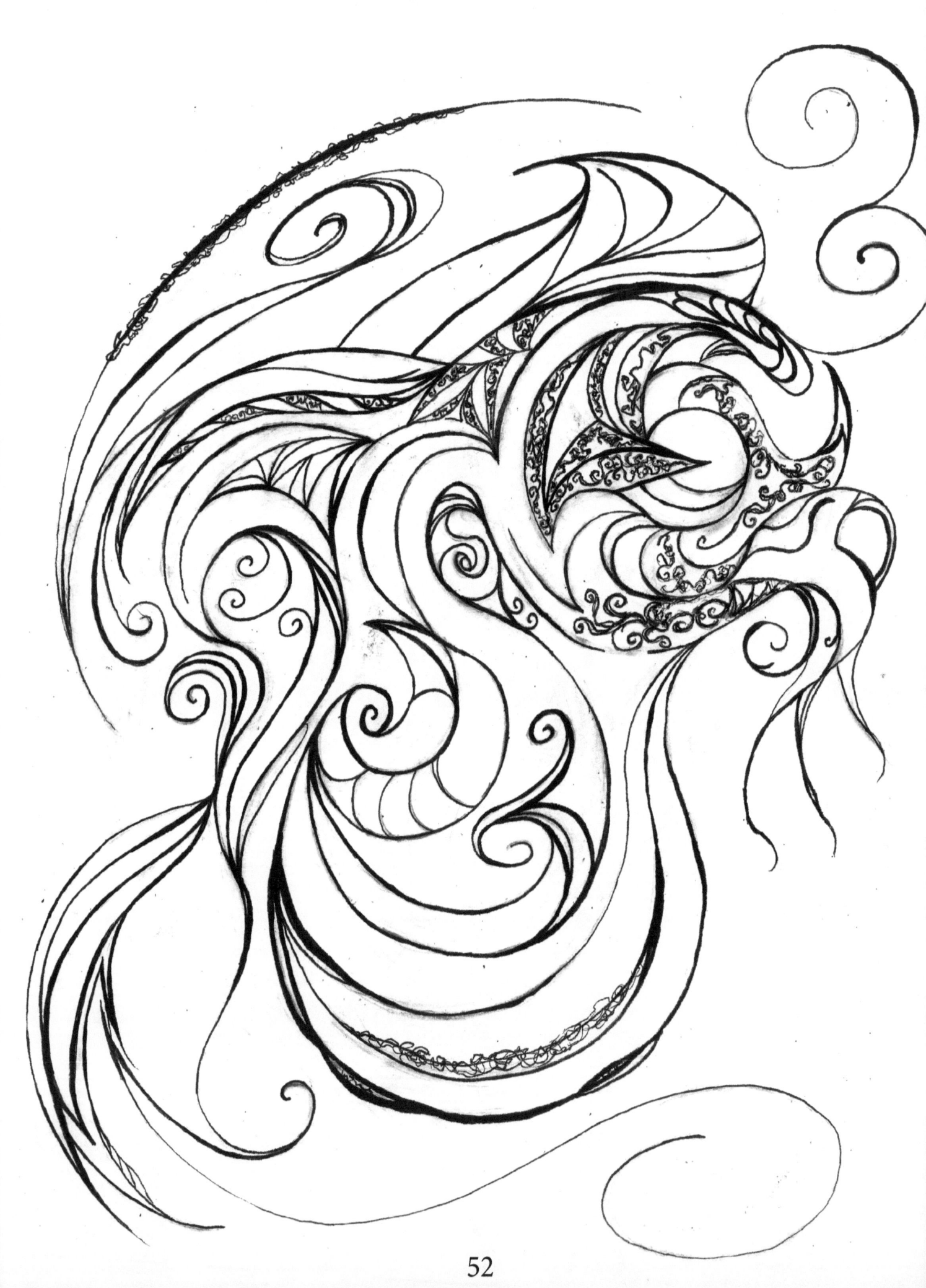

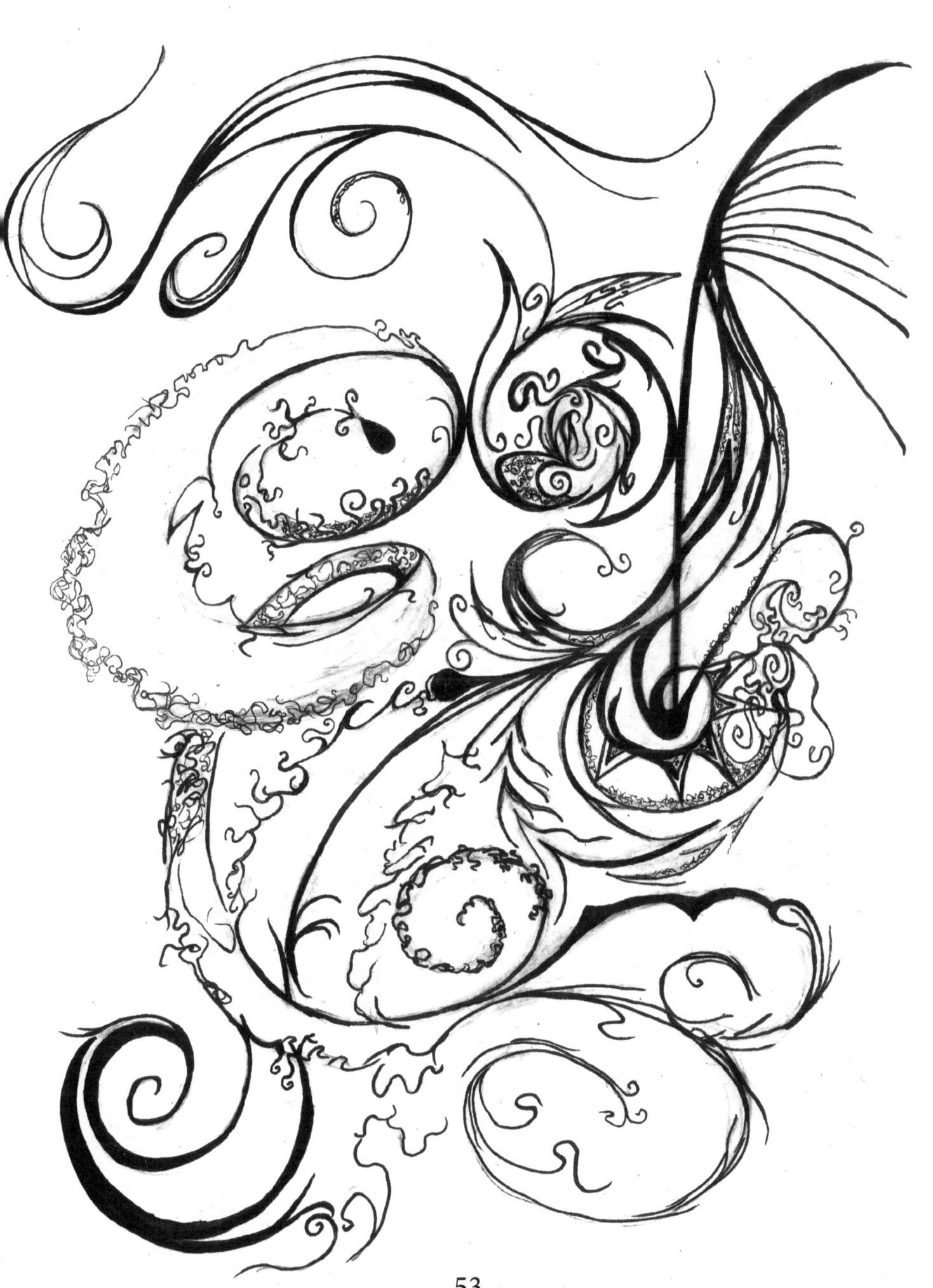

What's Eating Us?

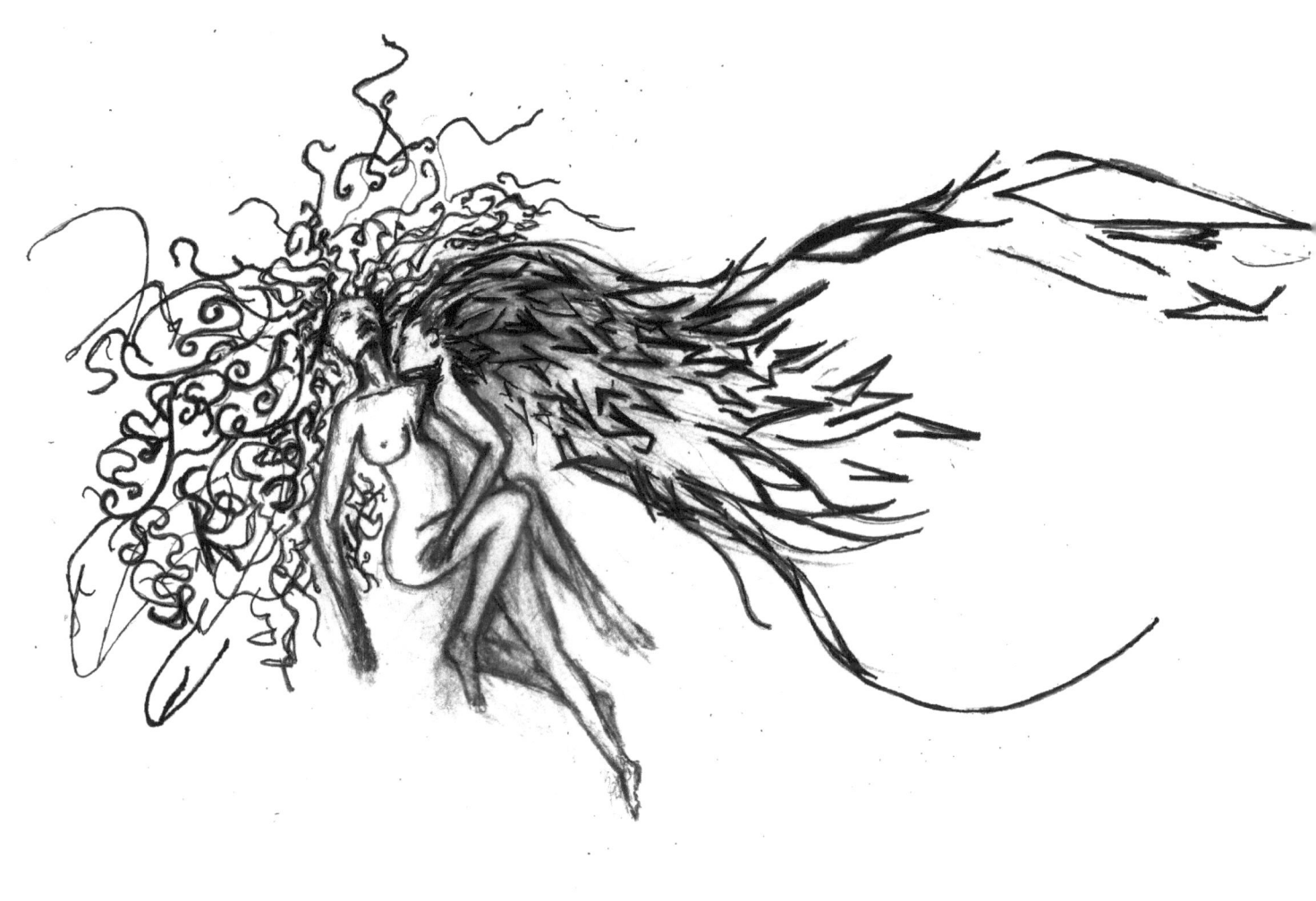

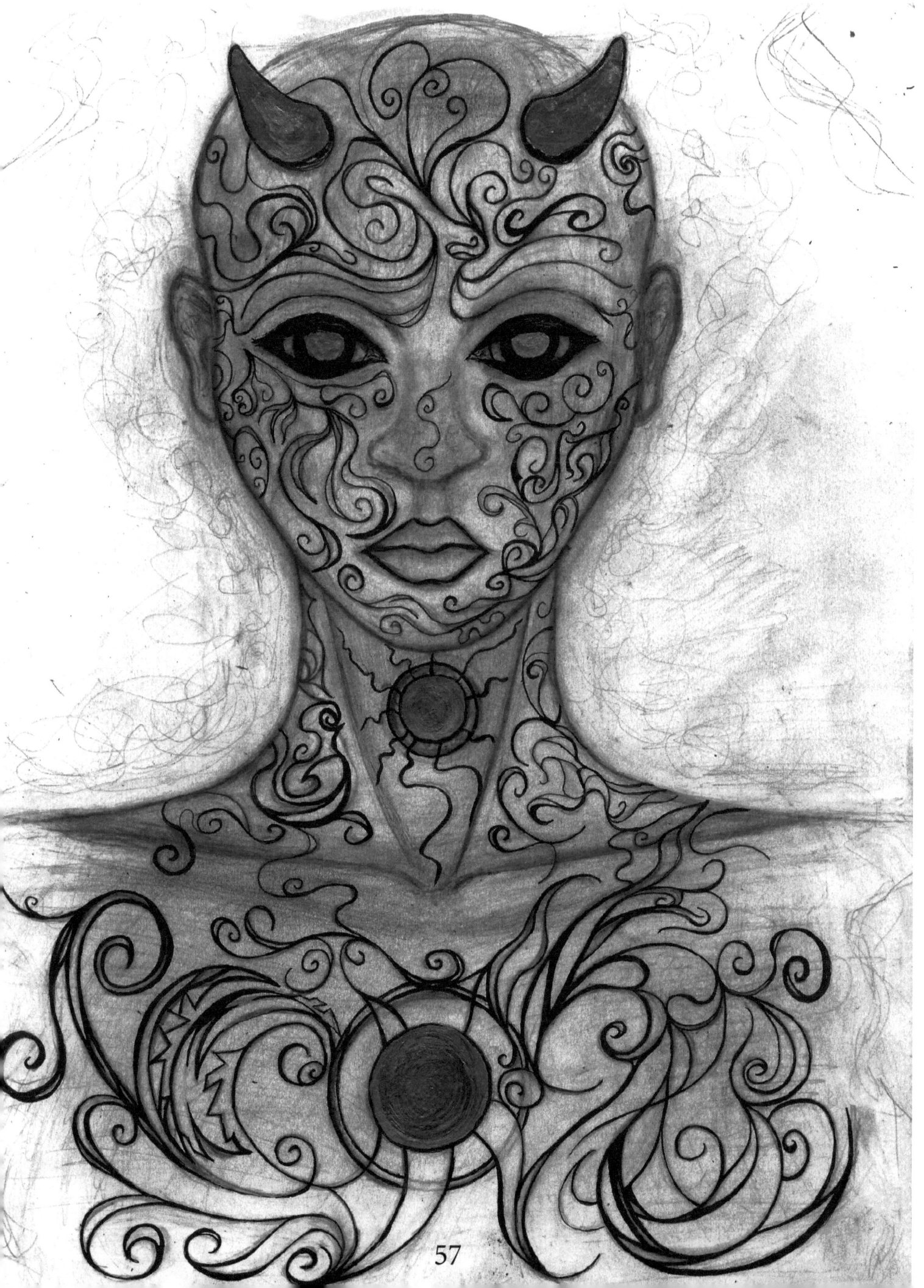

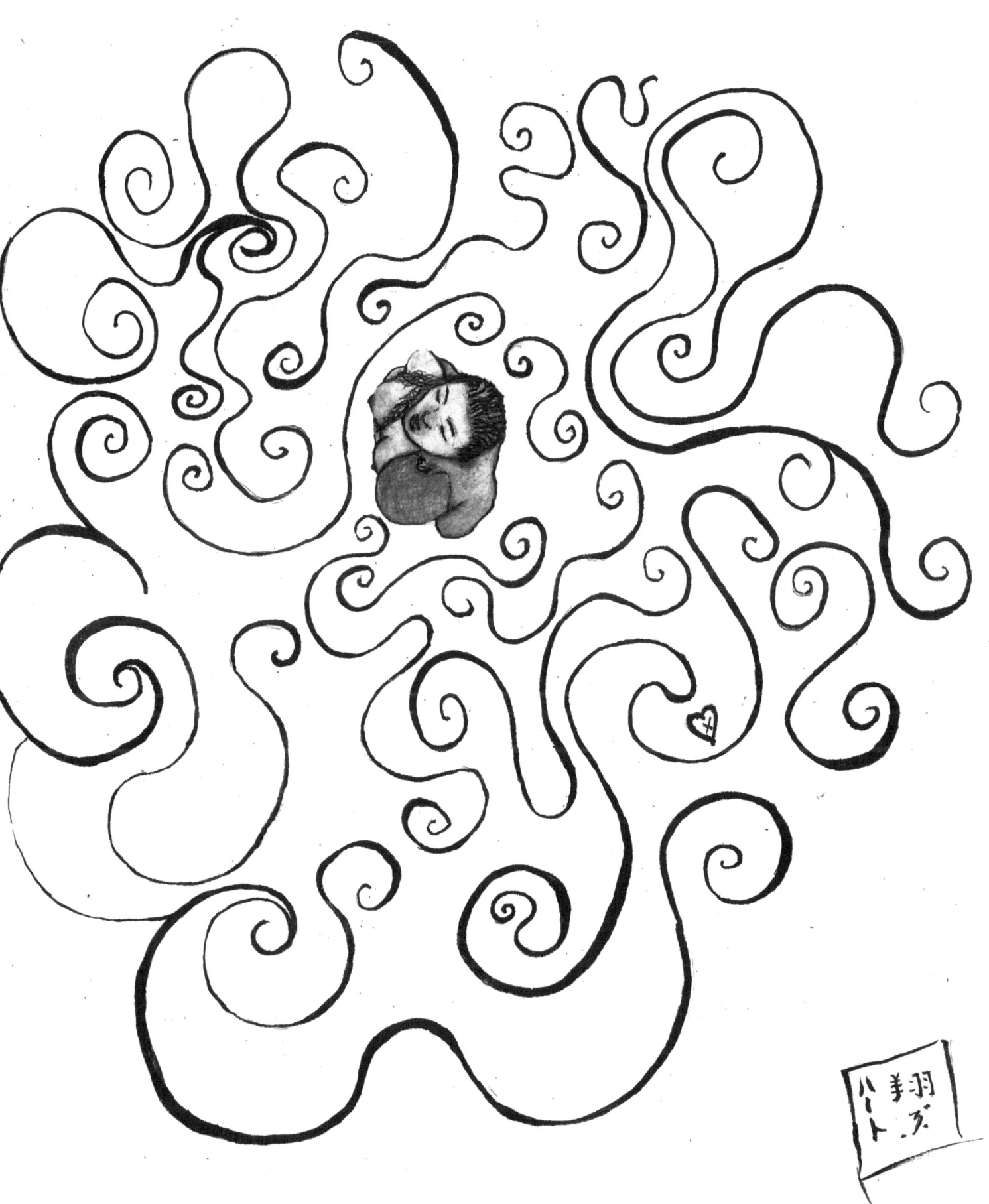

The Negatives
(Bonus Pages)

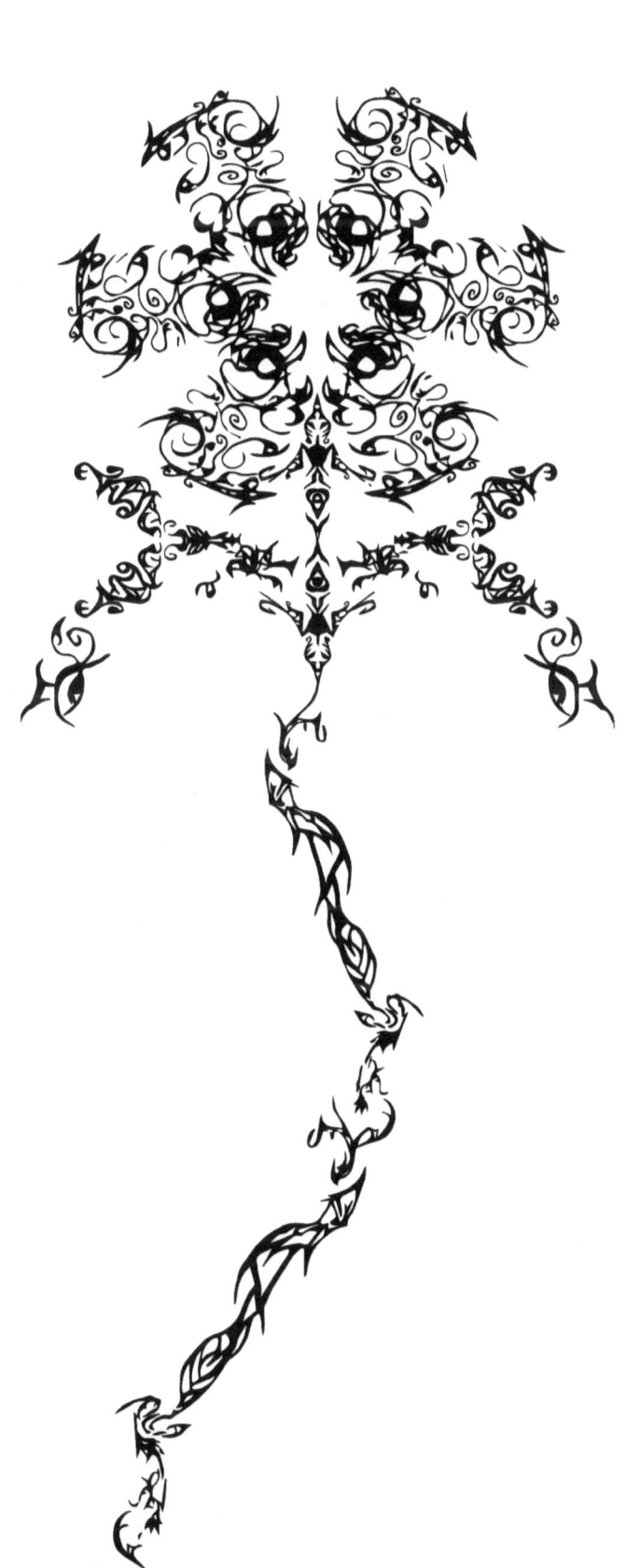

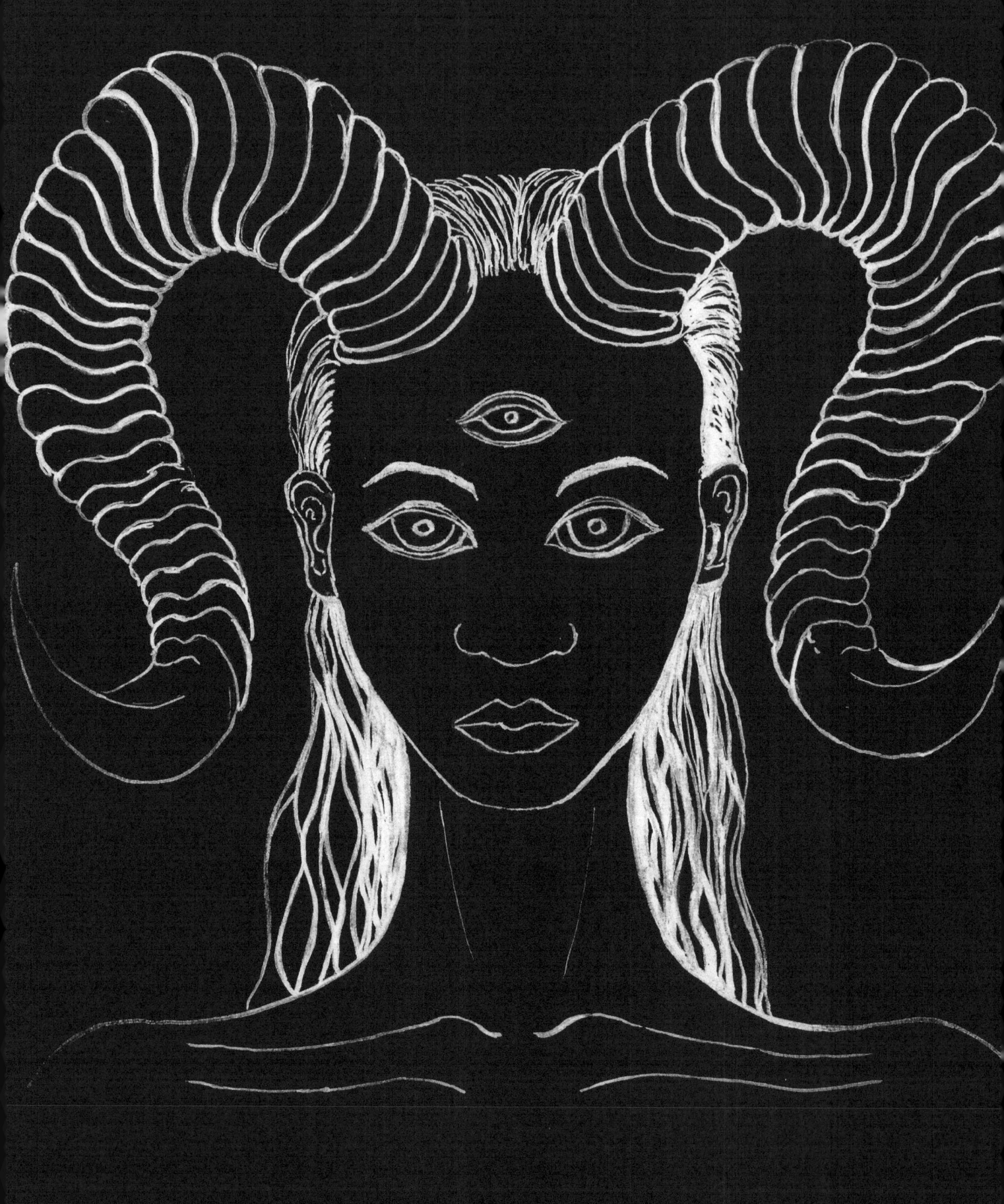

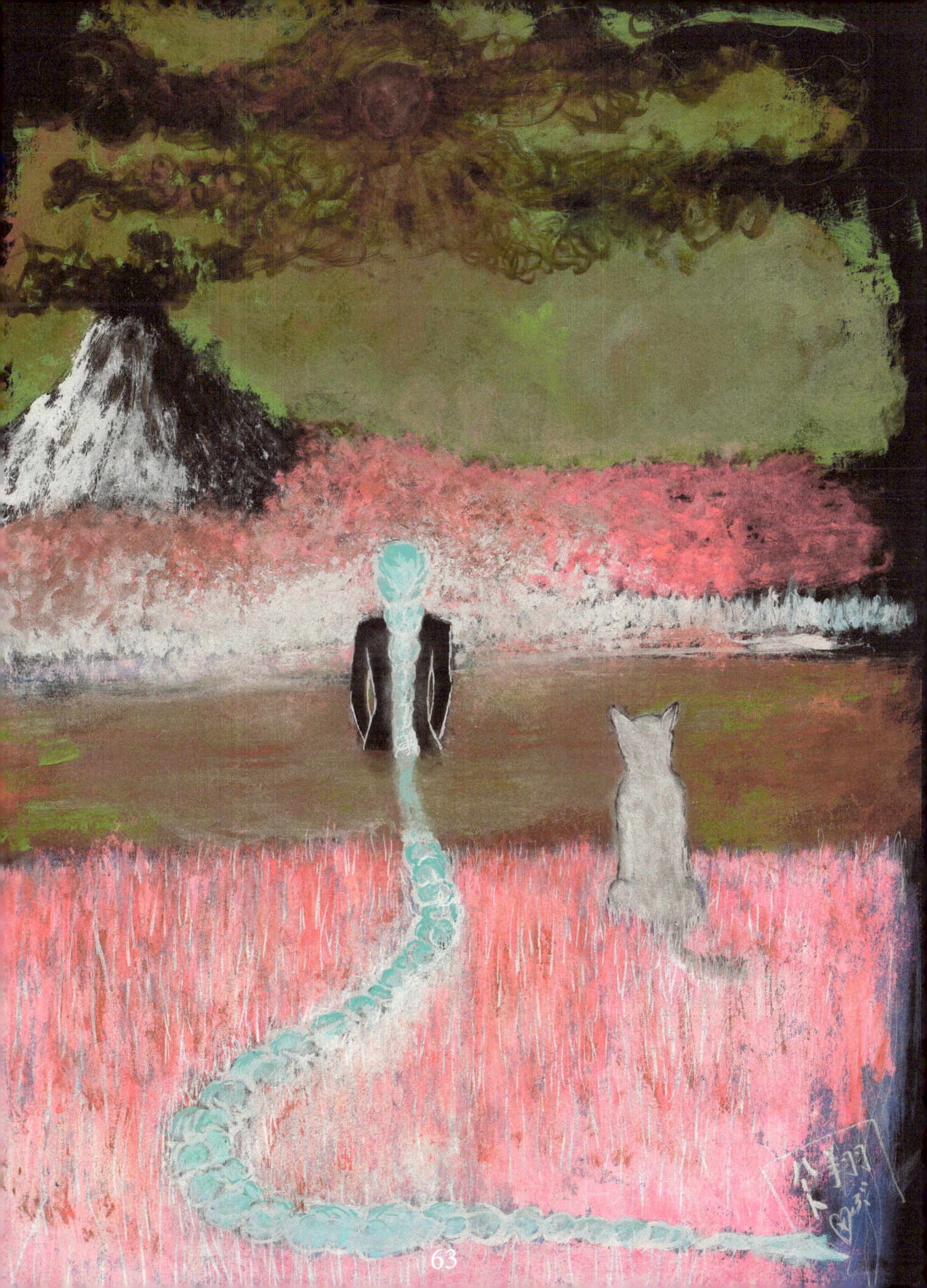

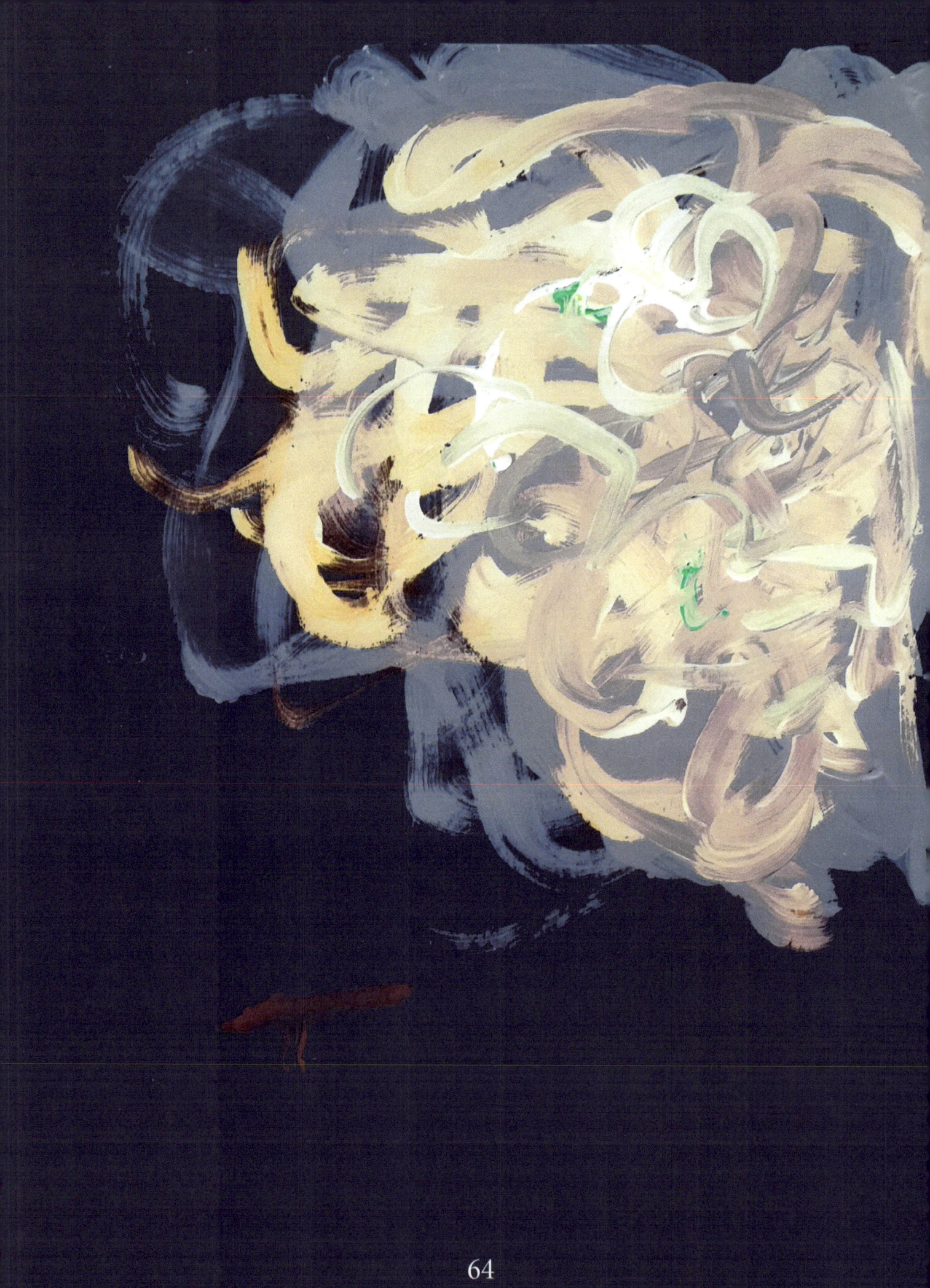

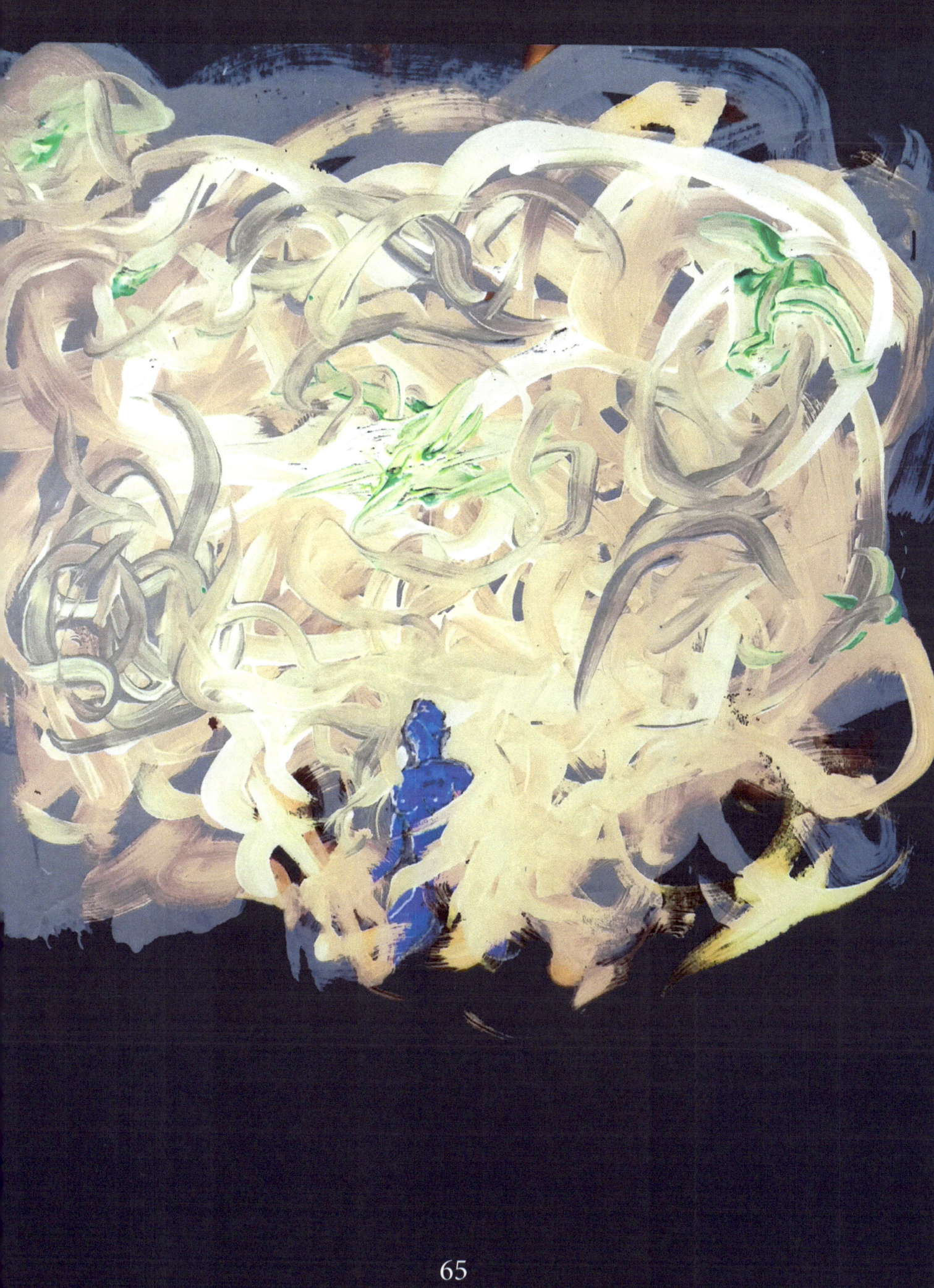

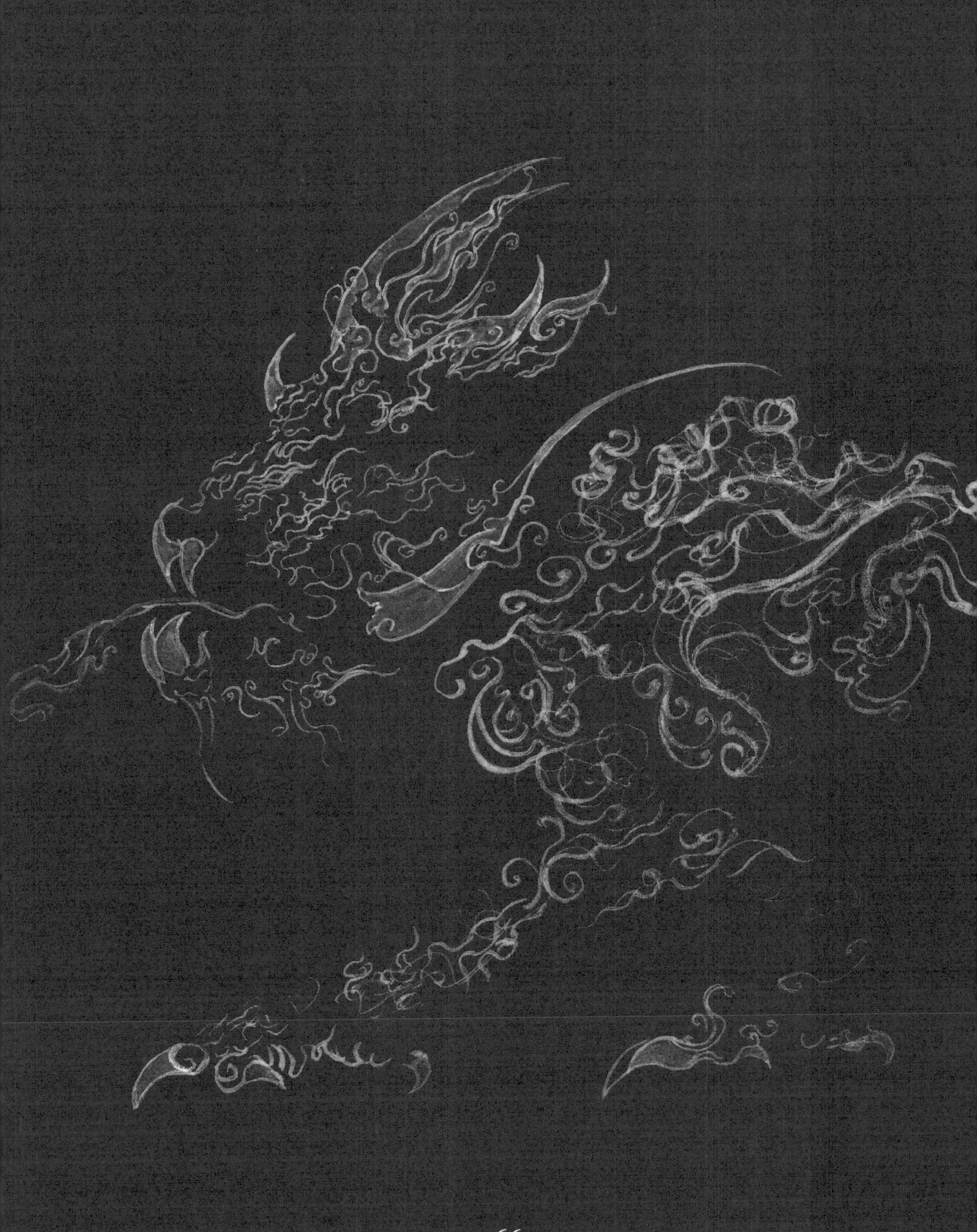

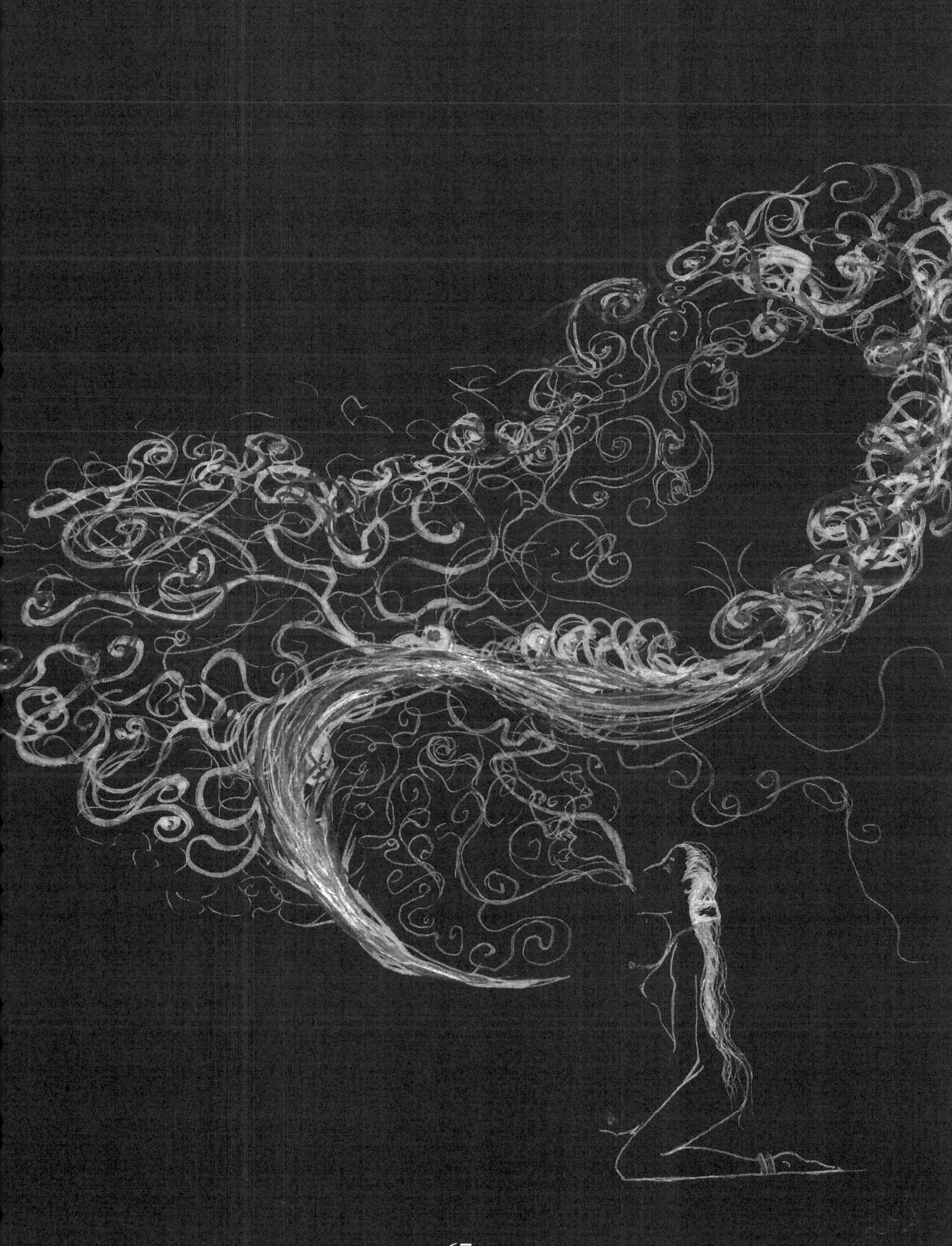

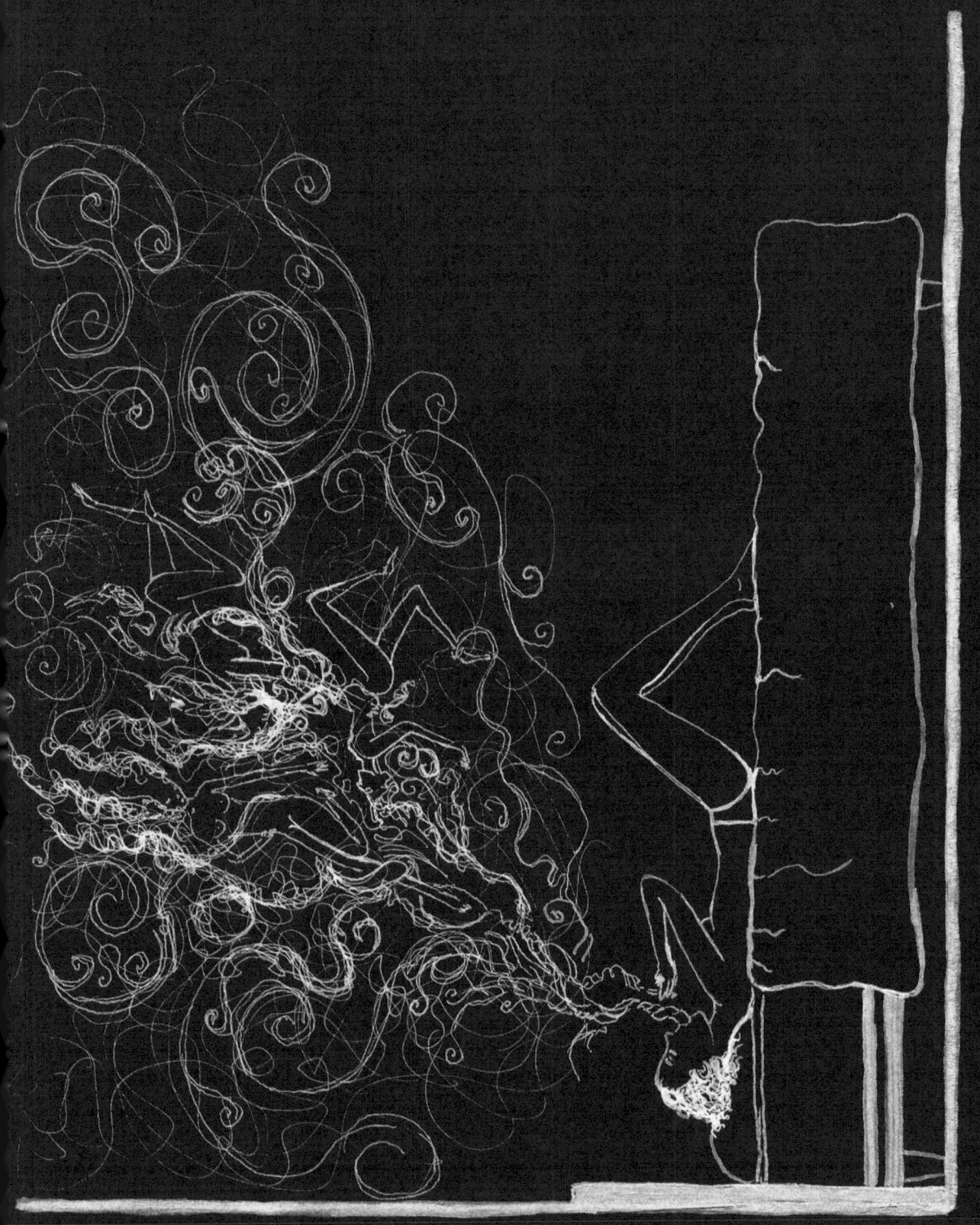

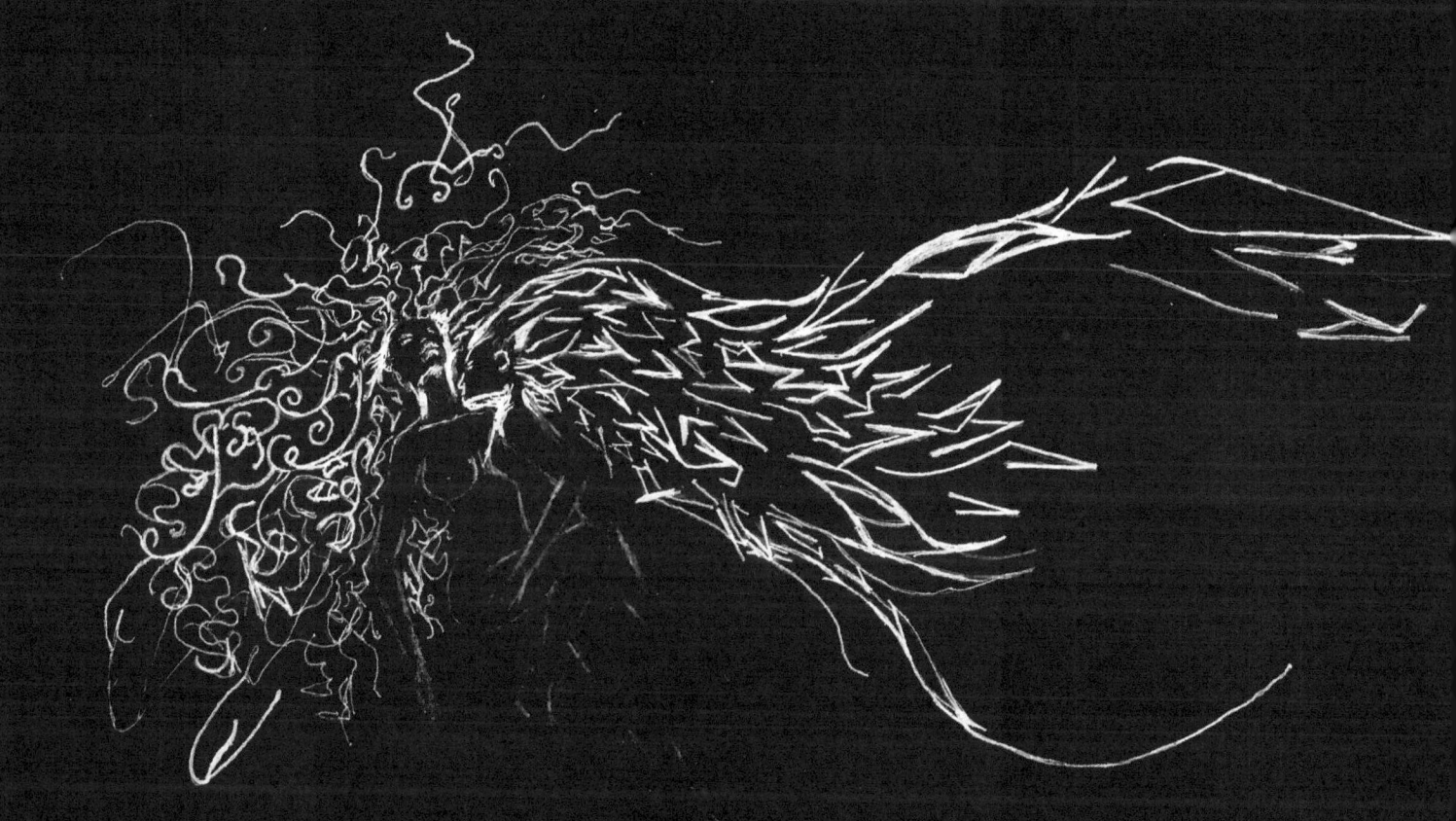

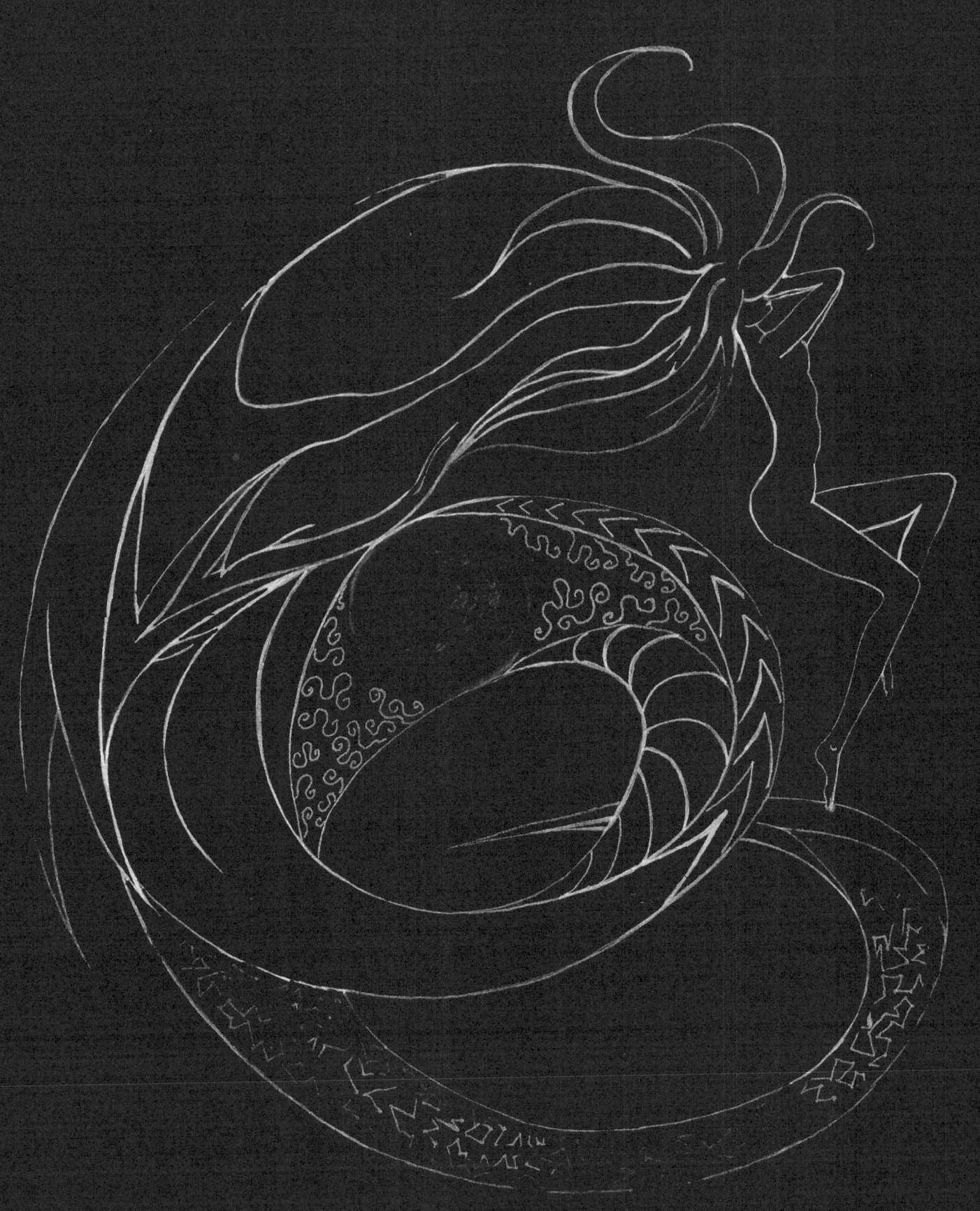

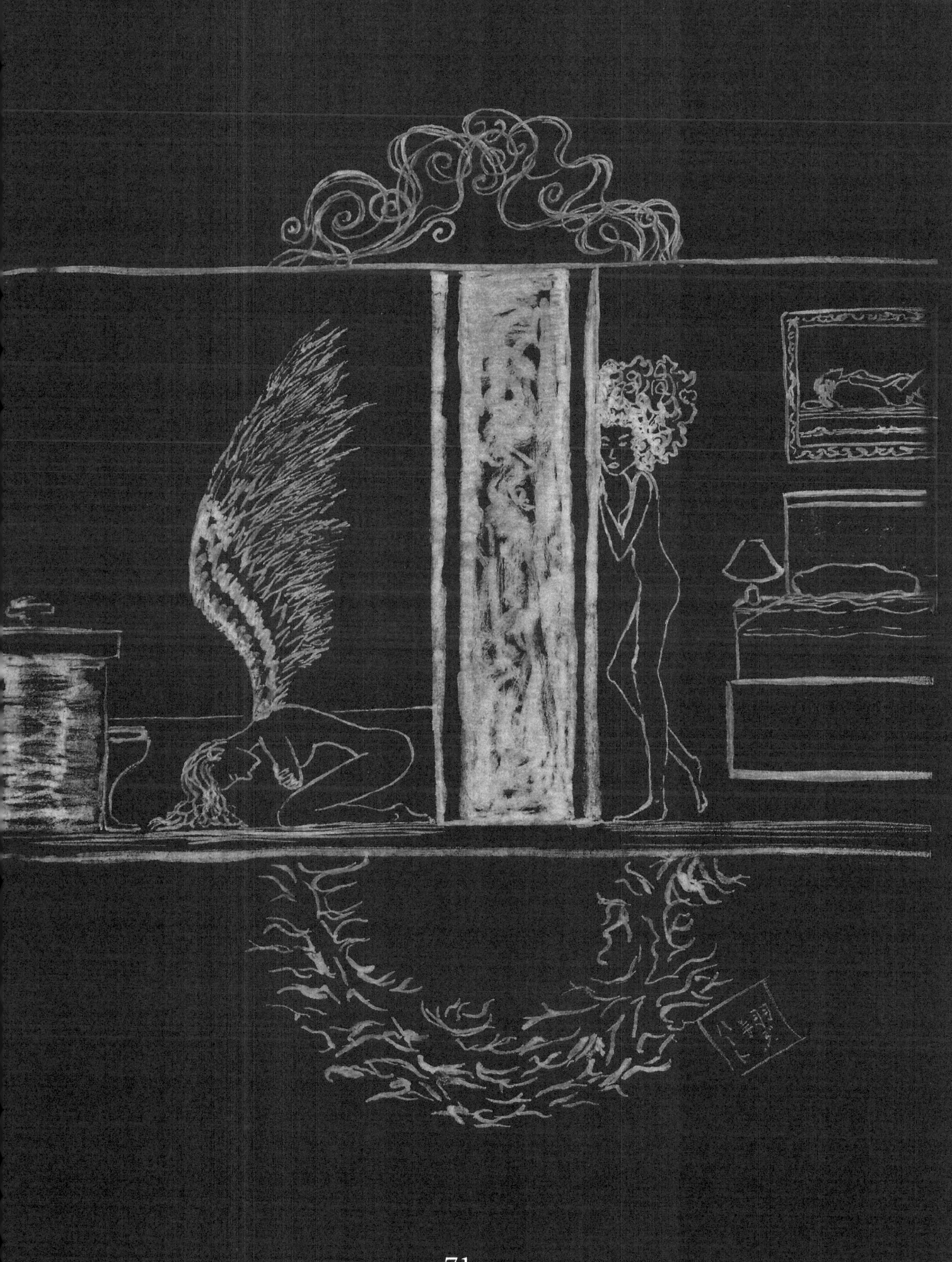

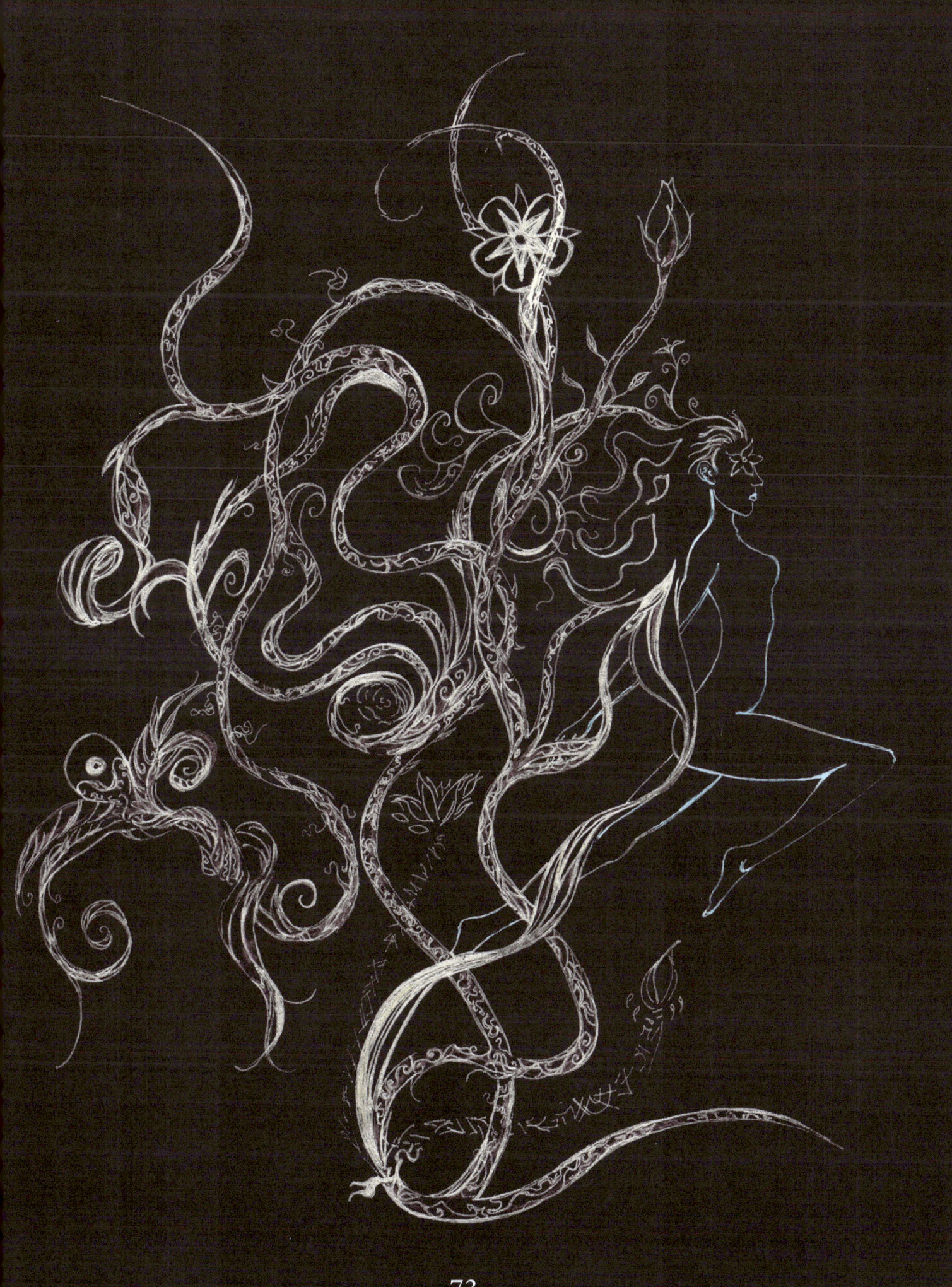

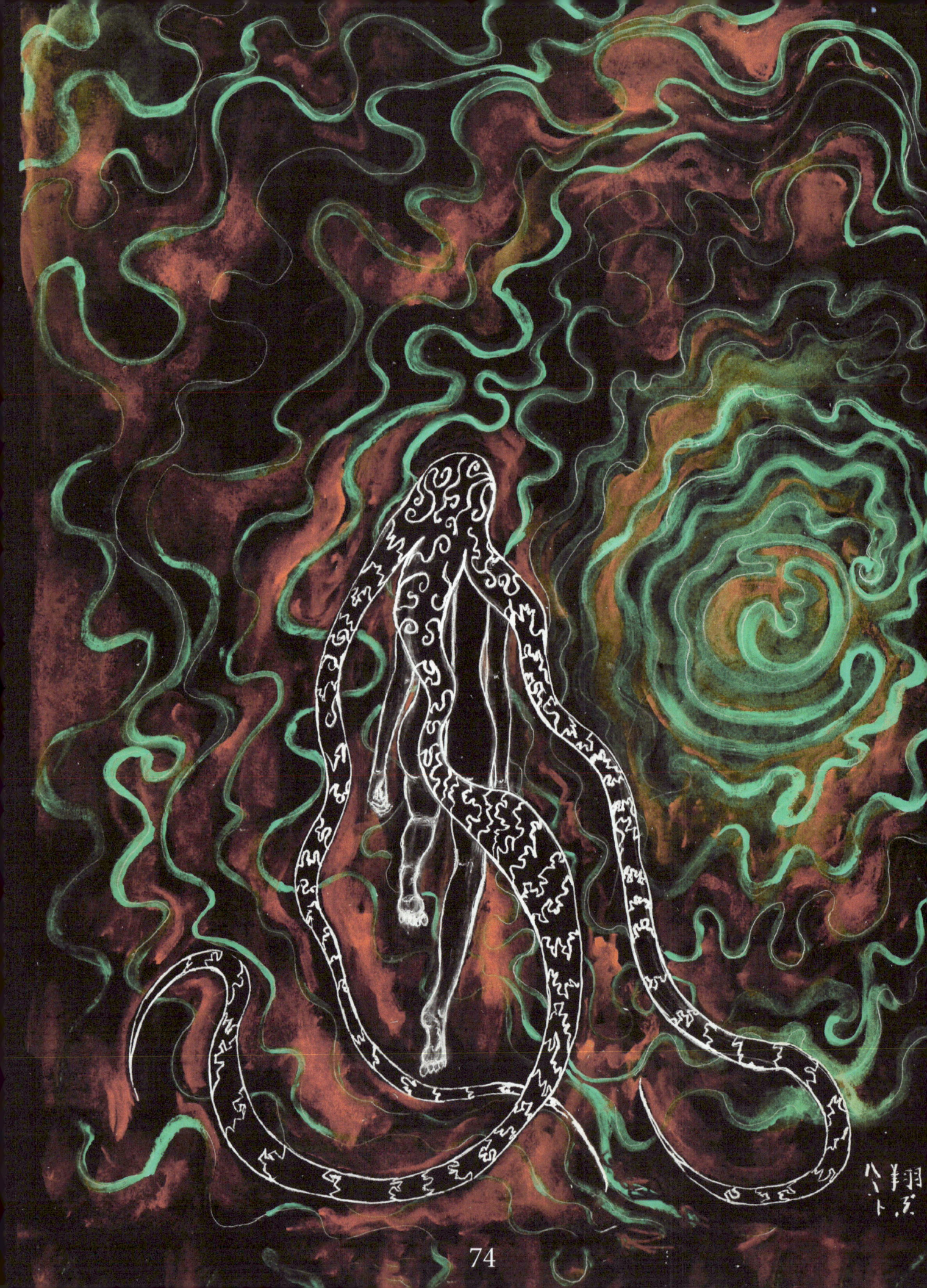

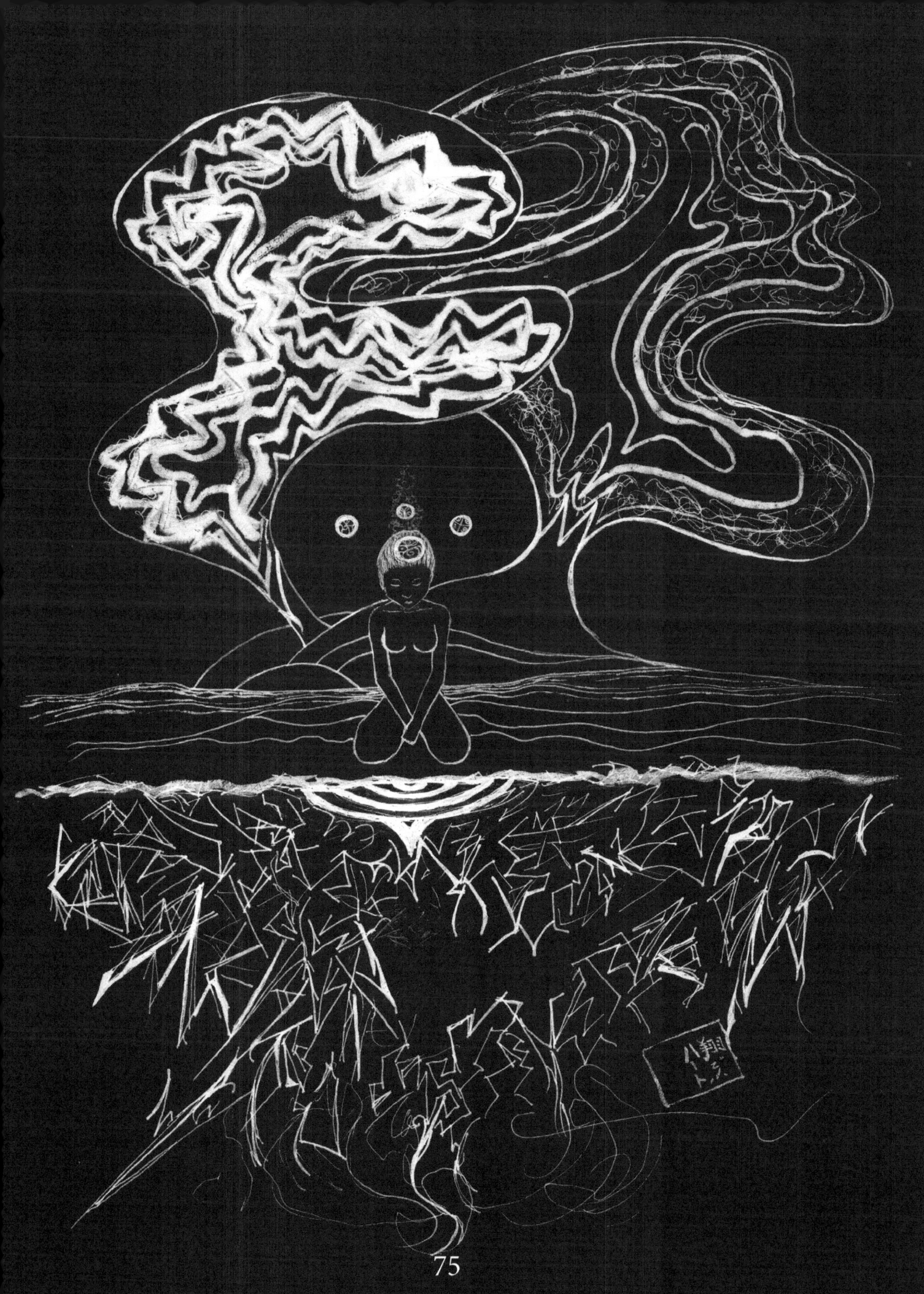

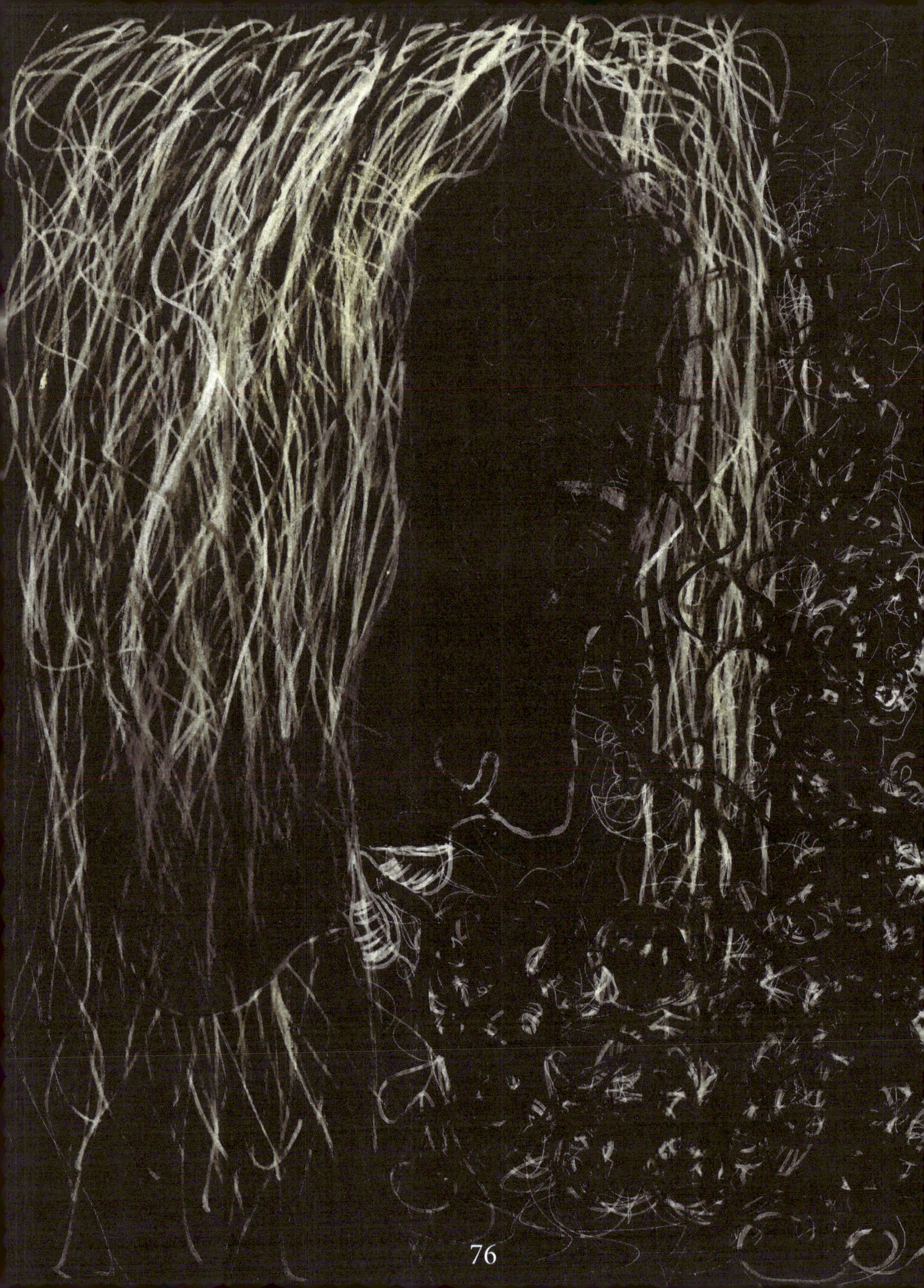

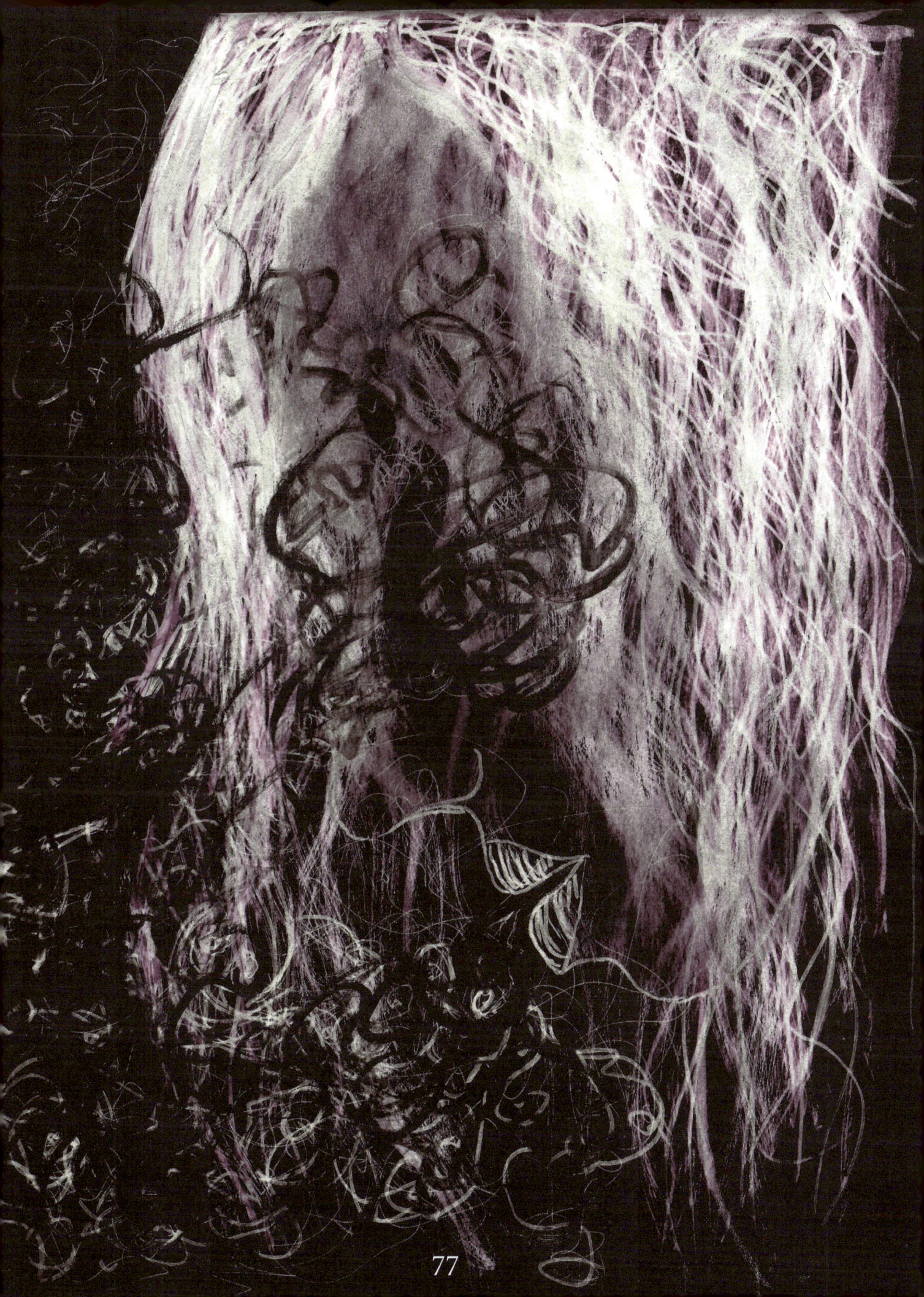

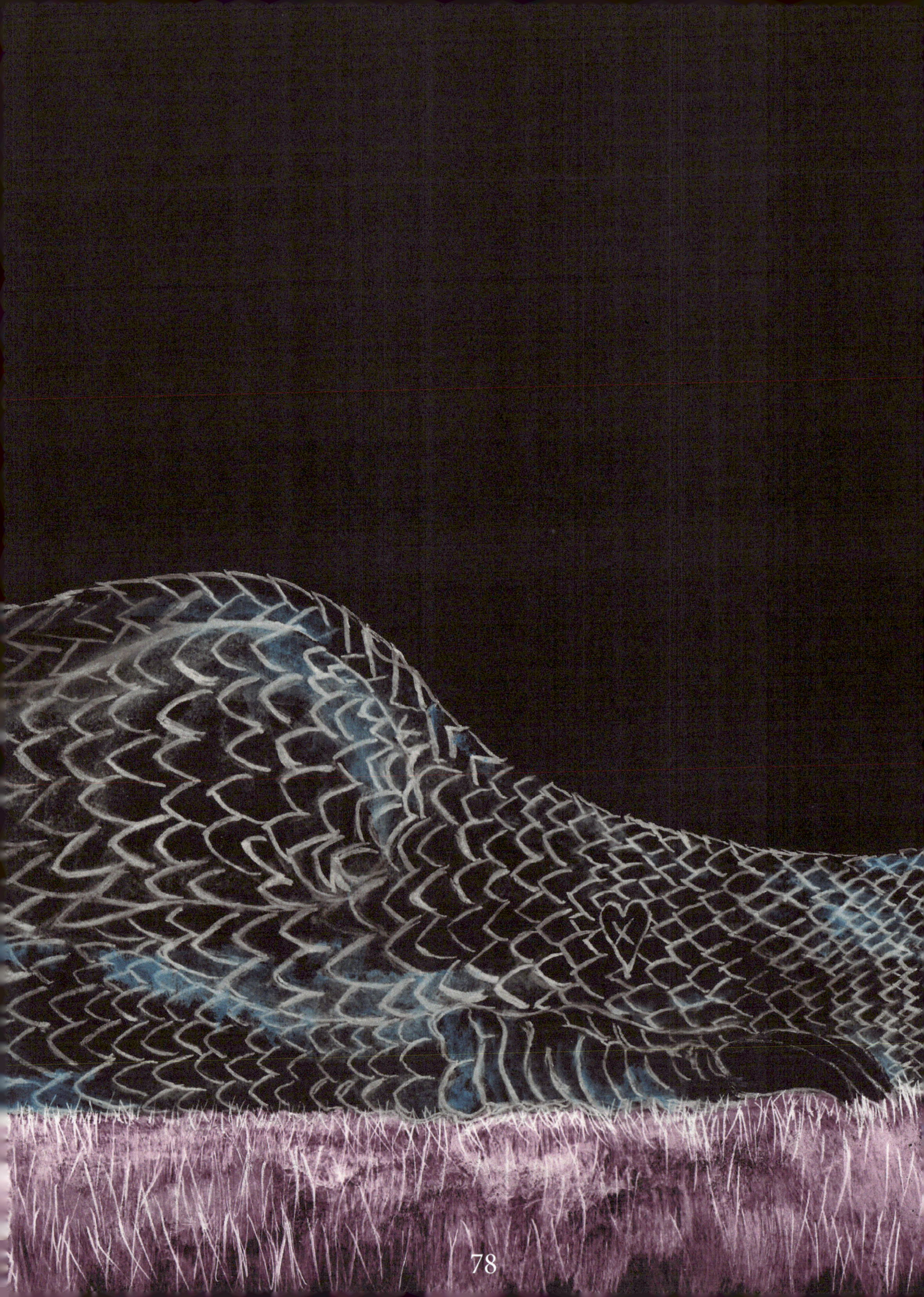

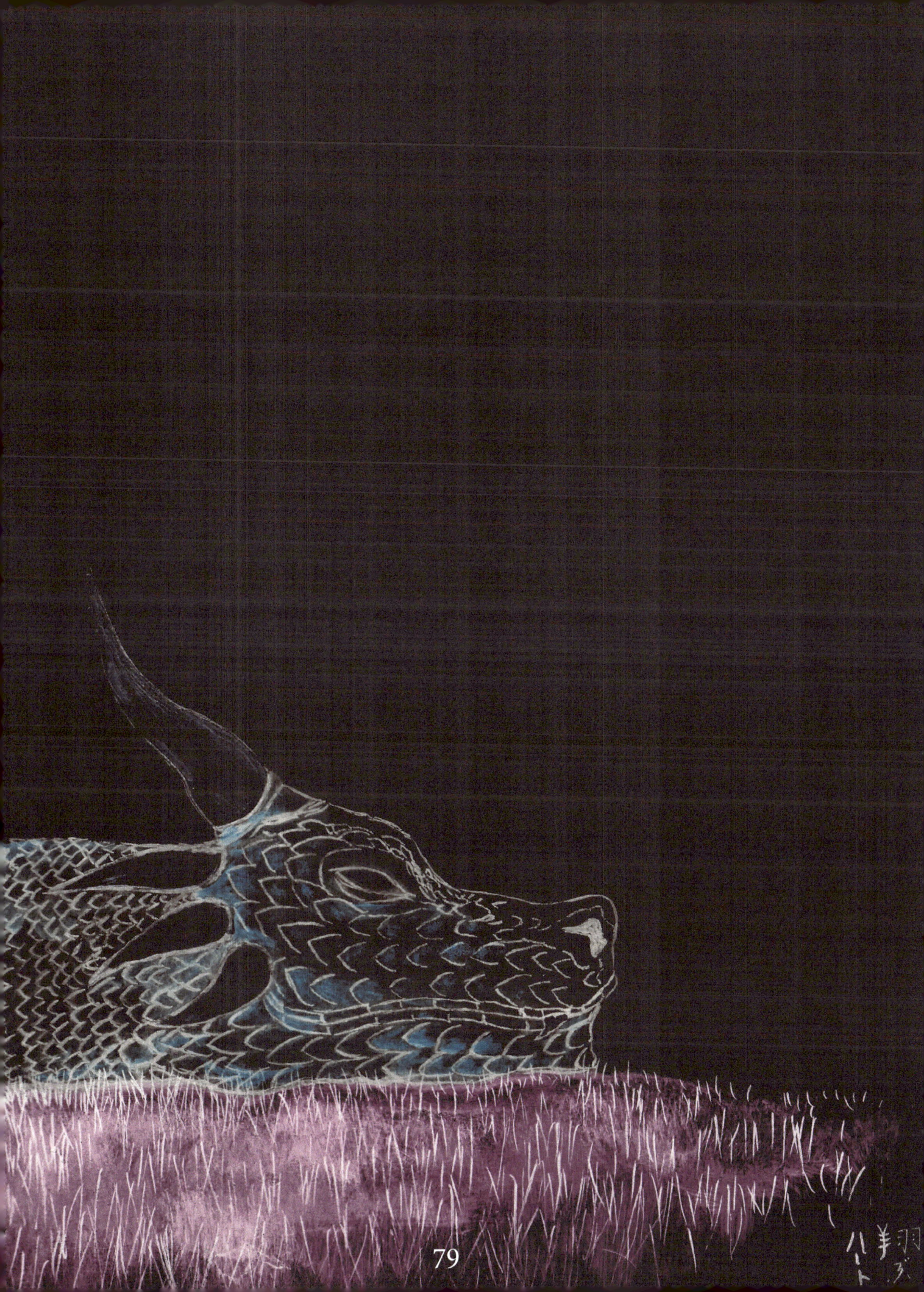

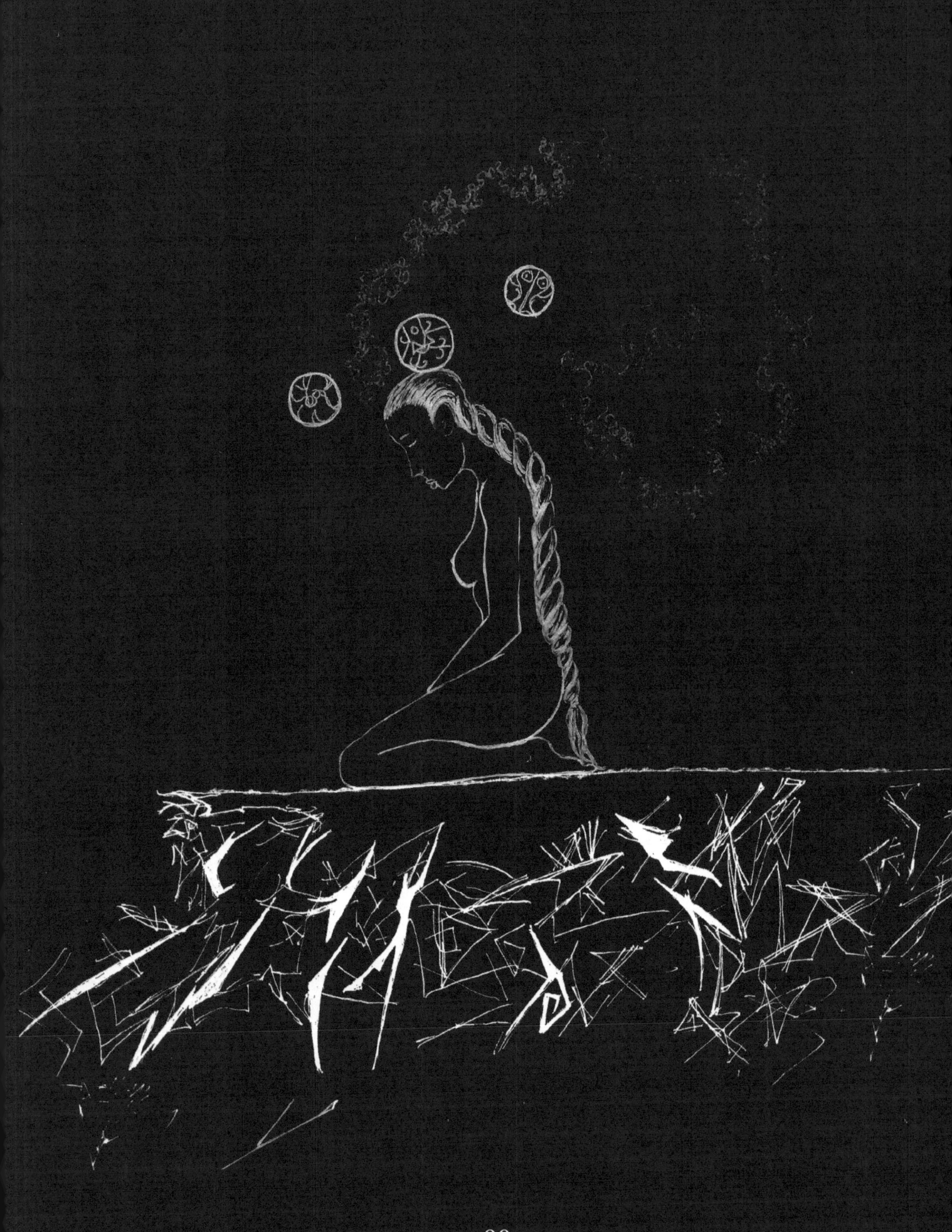

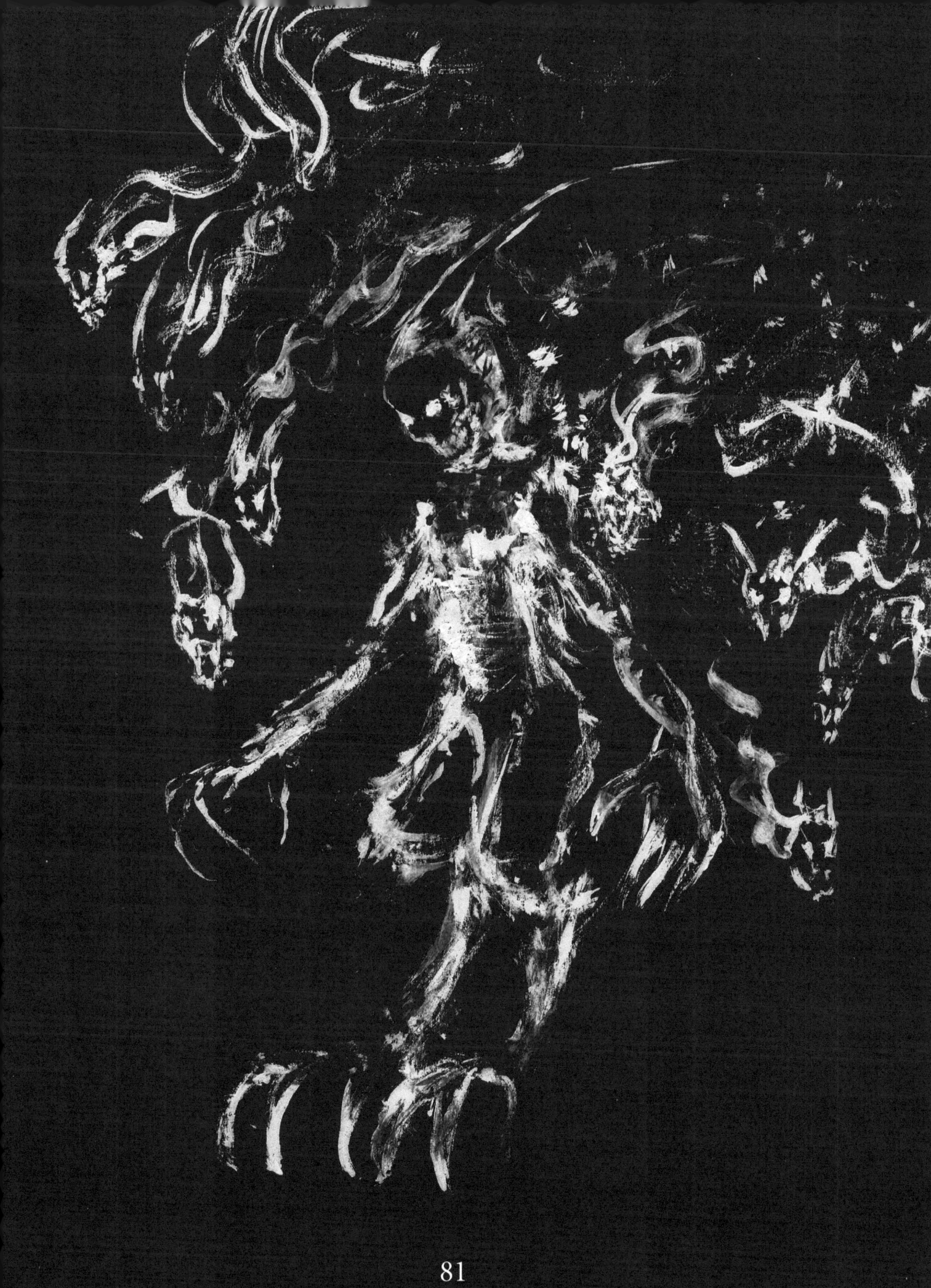

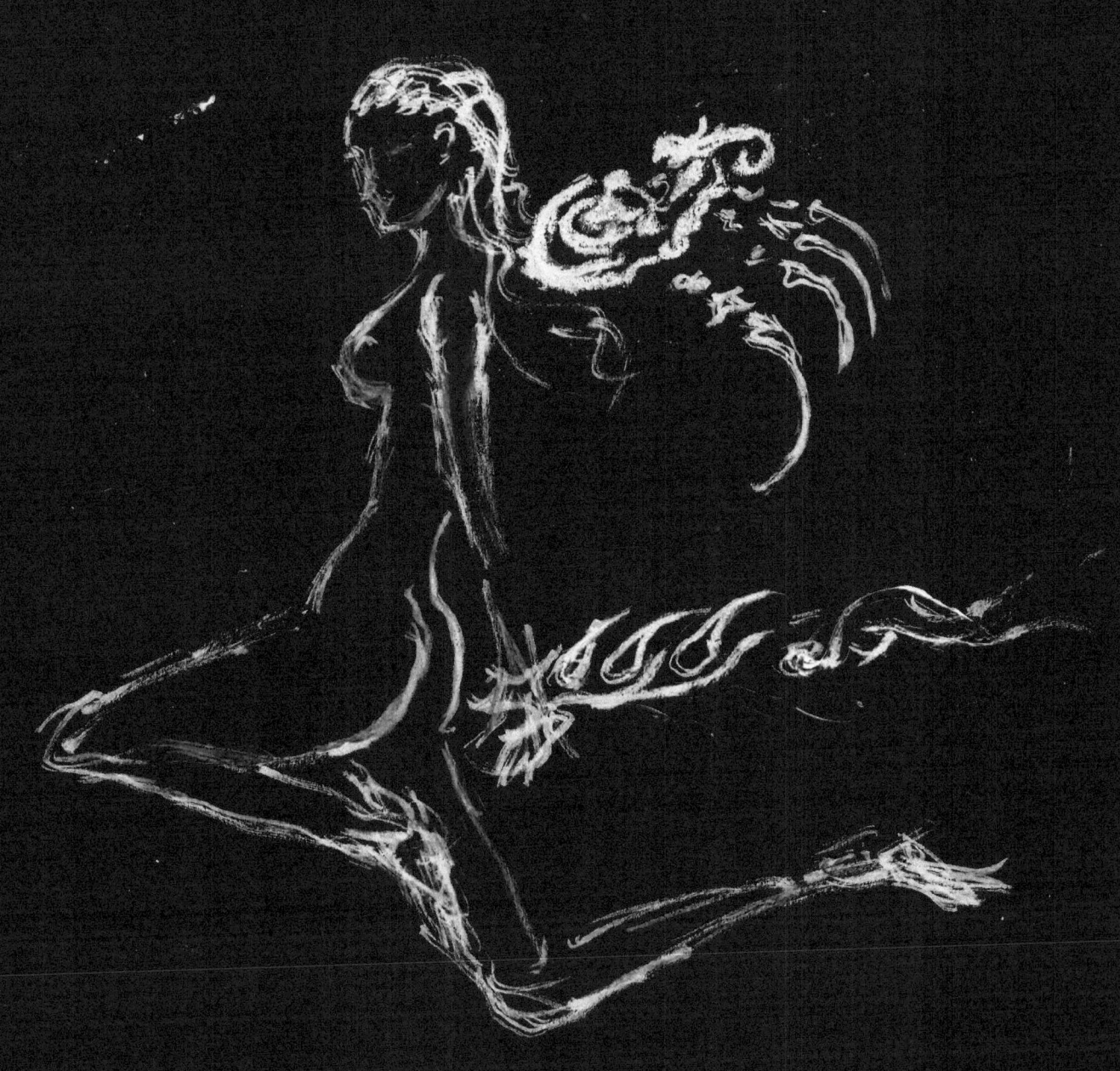

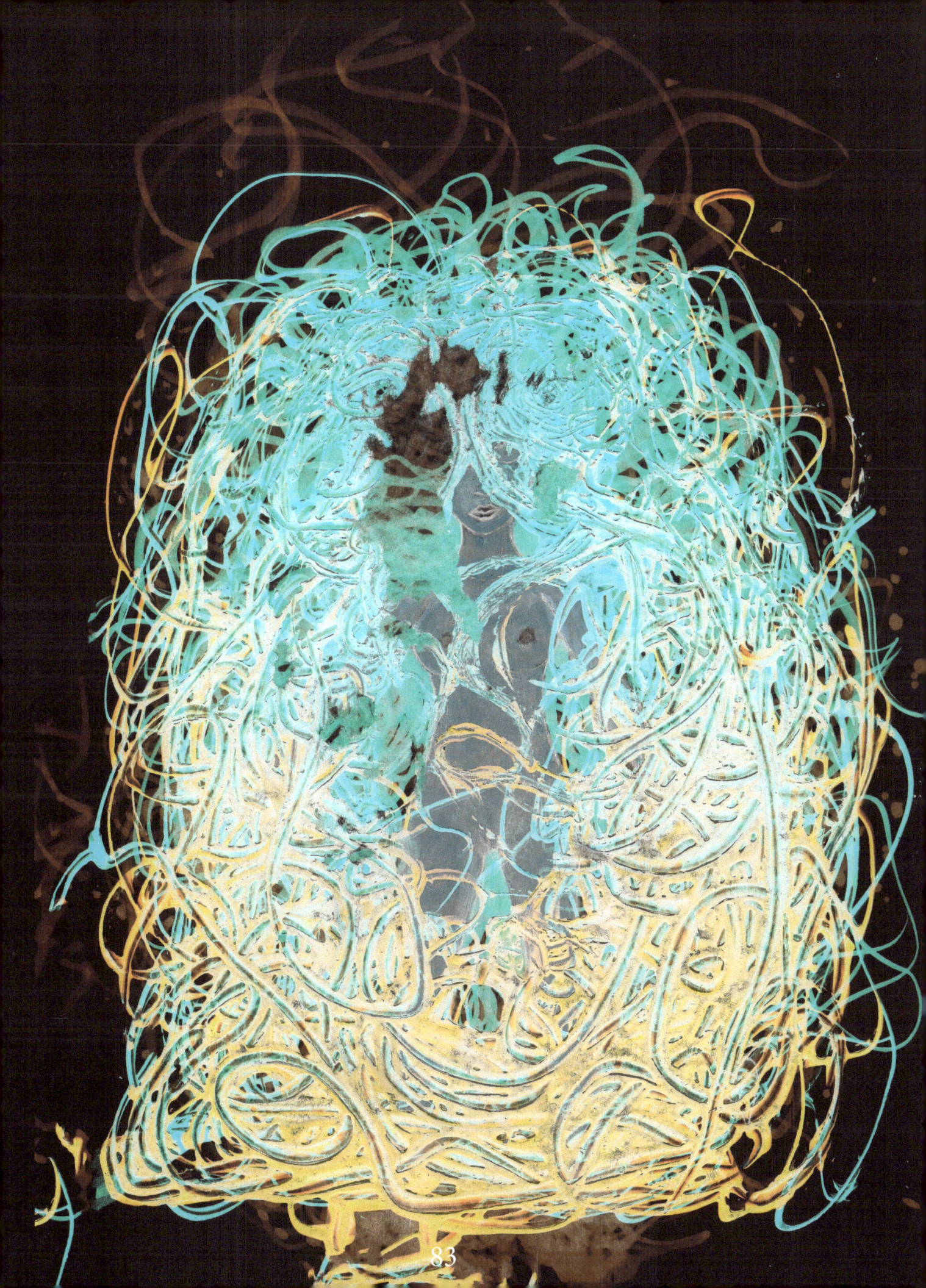

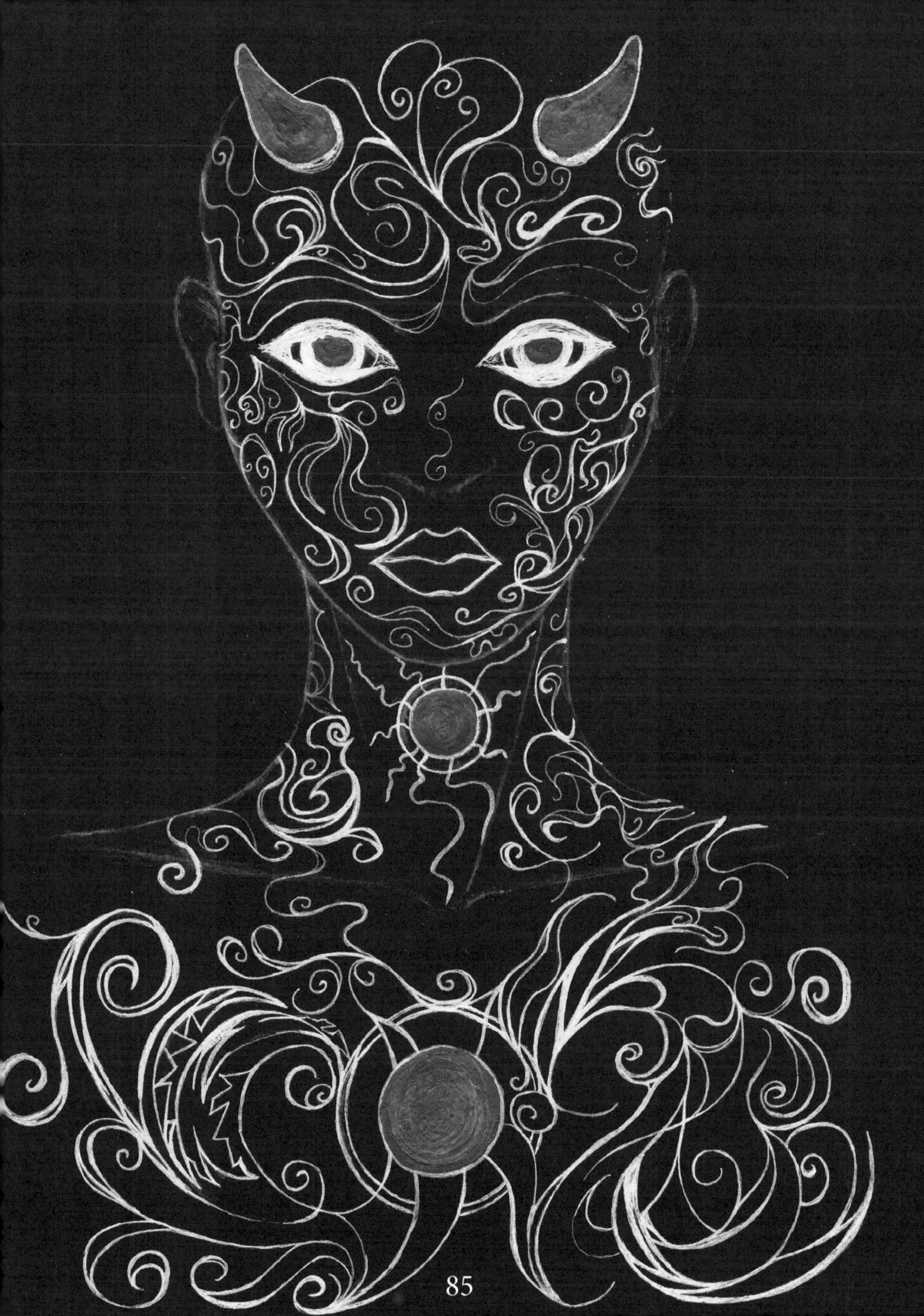

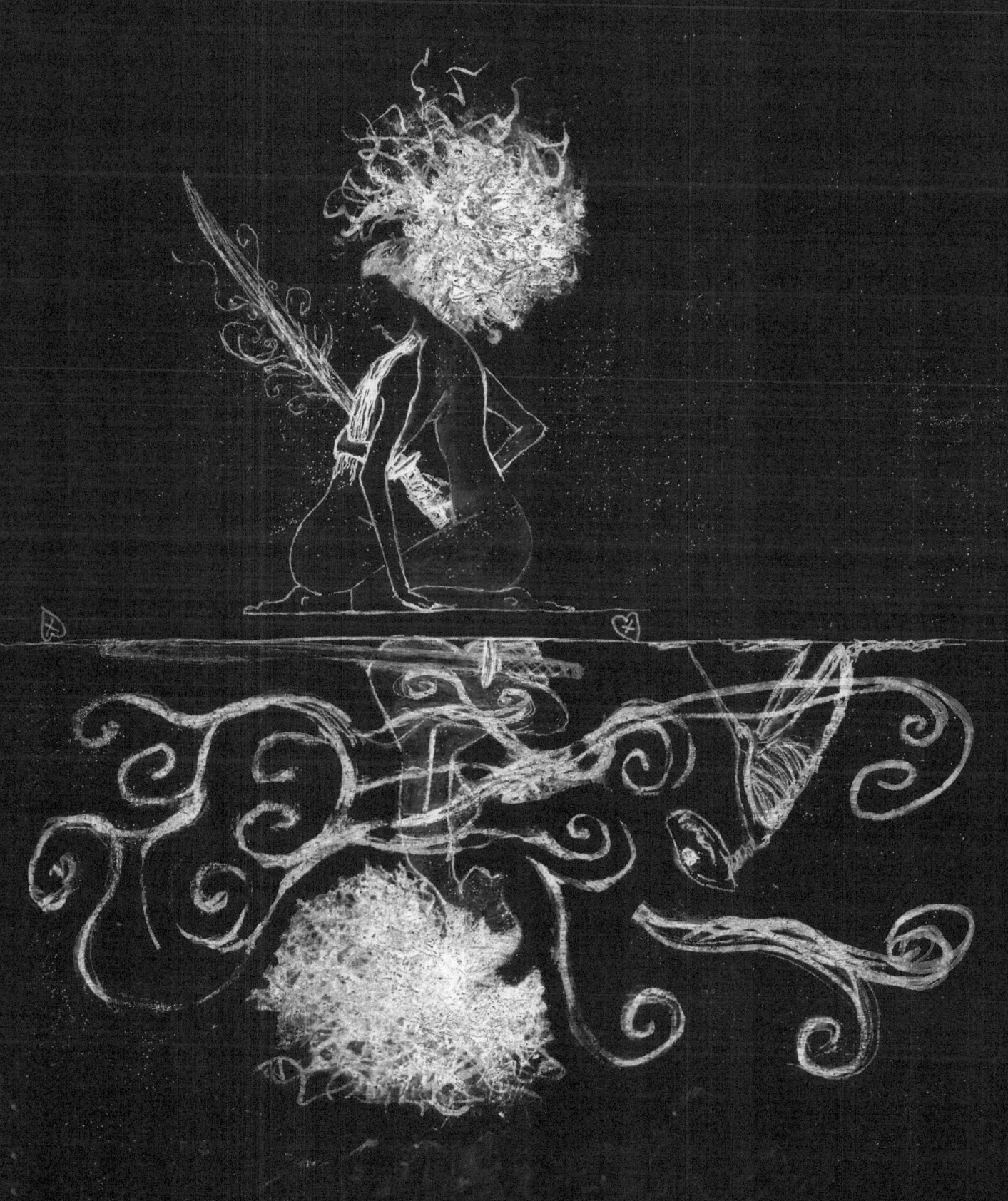

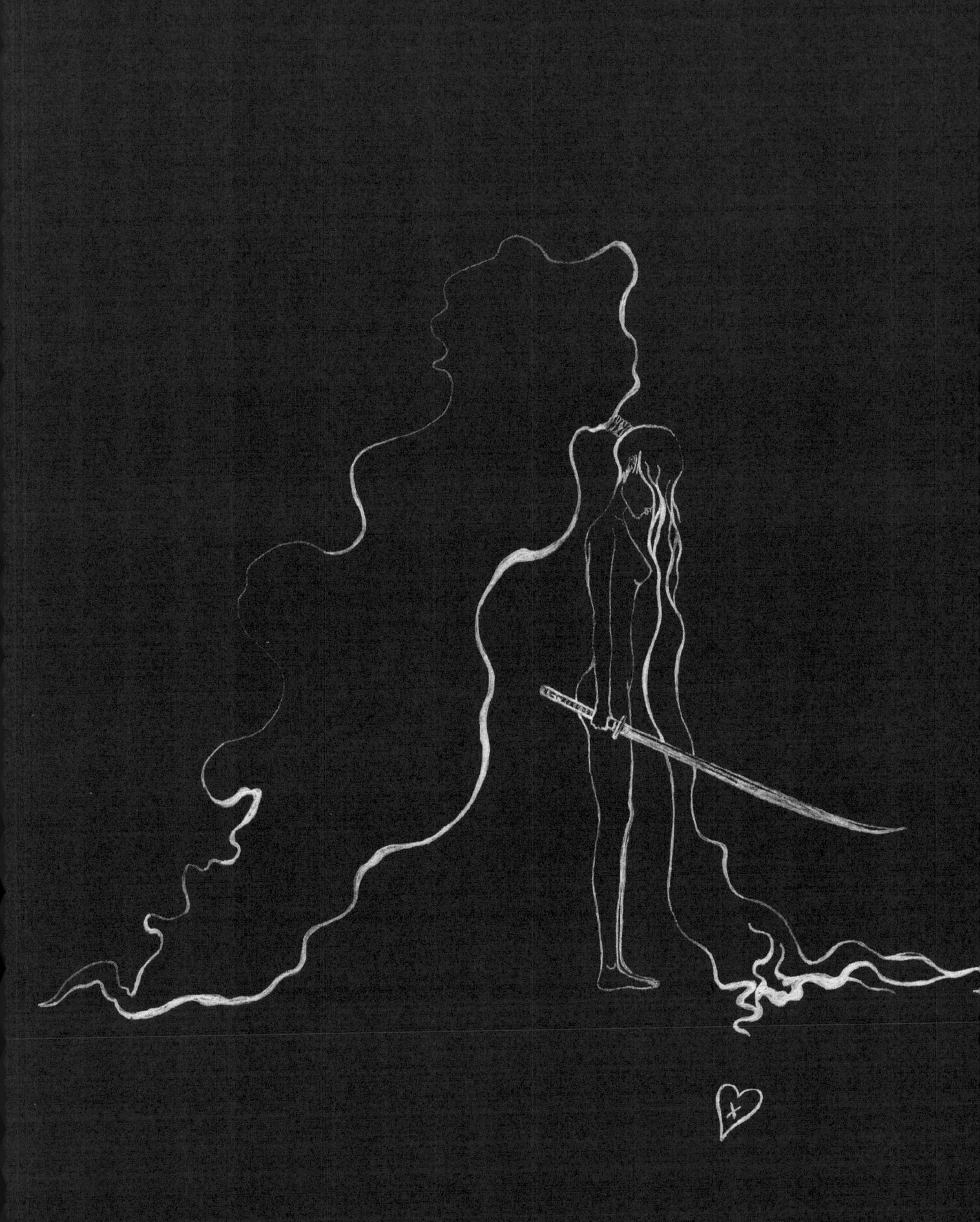

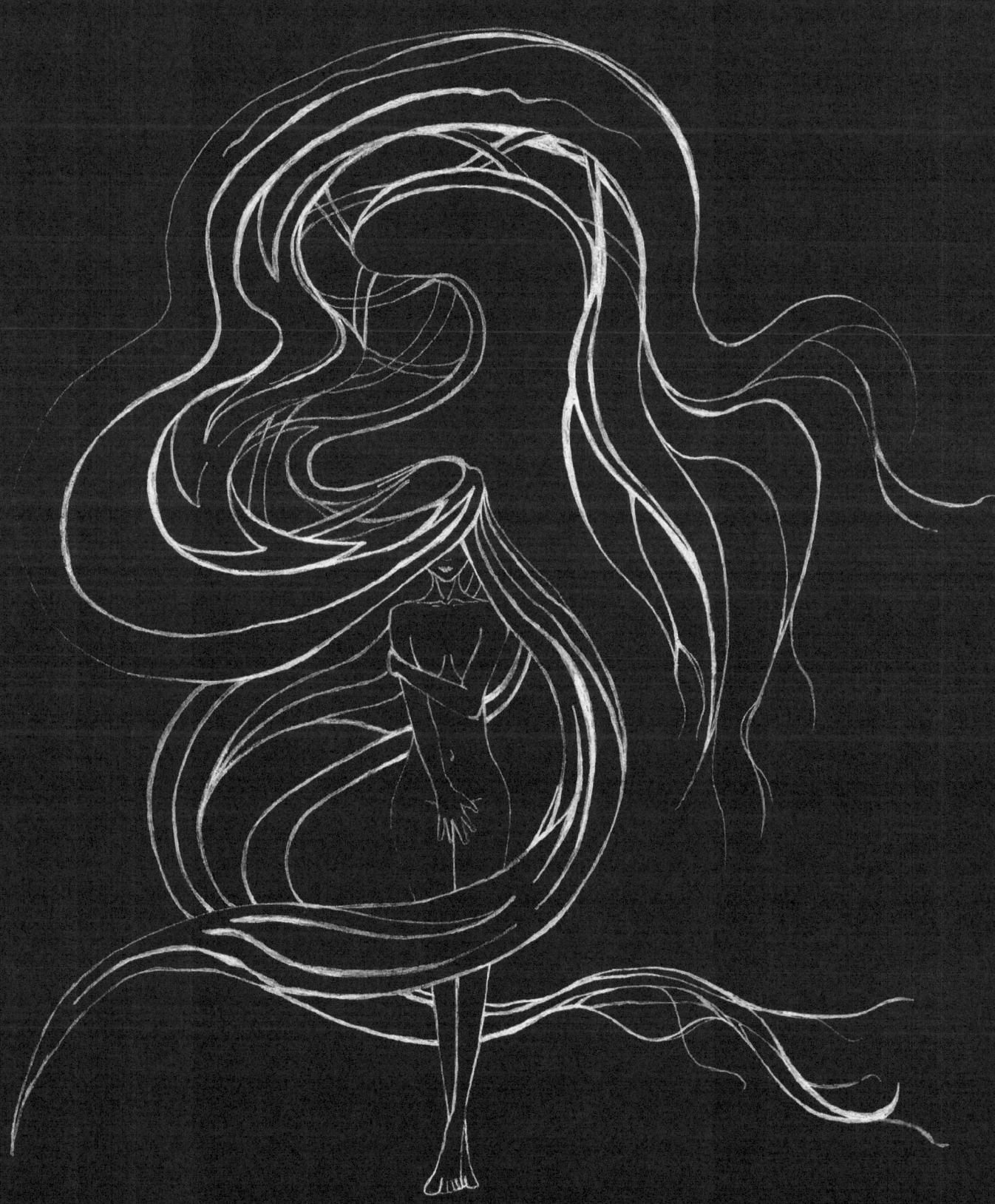

What if this is god?
What if she is god?

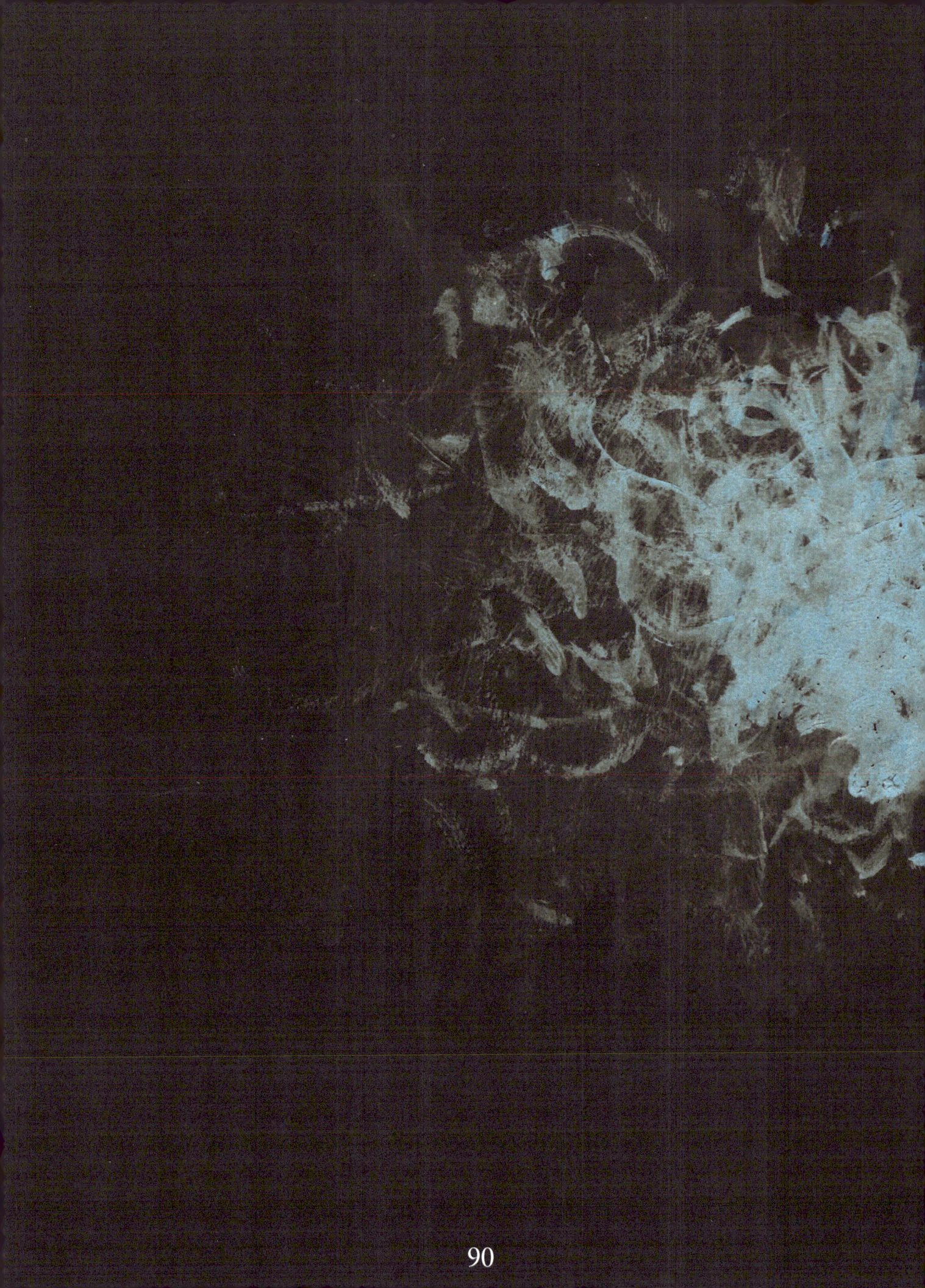

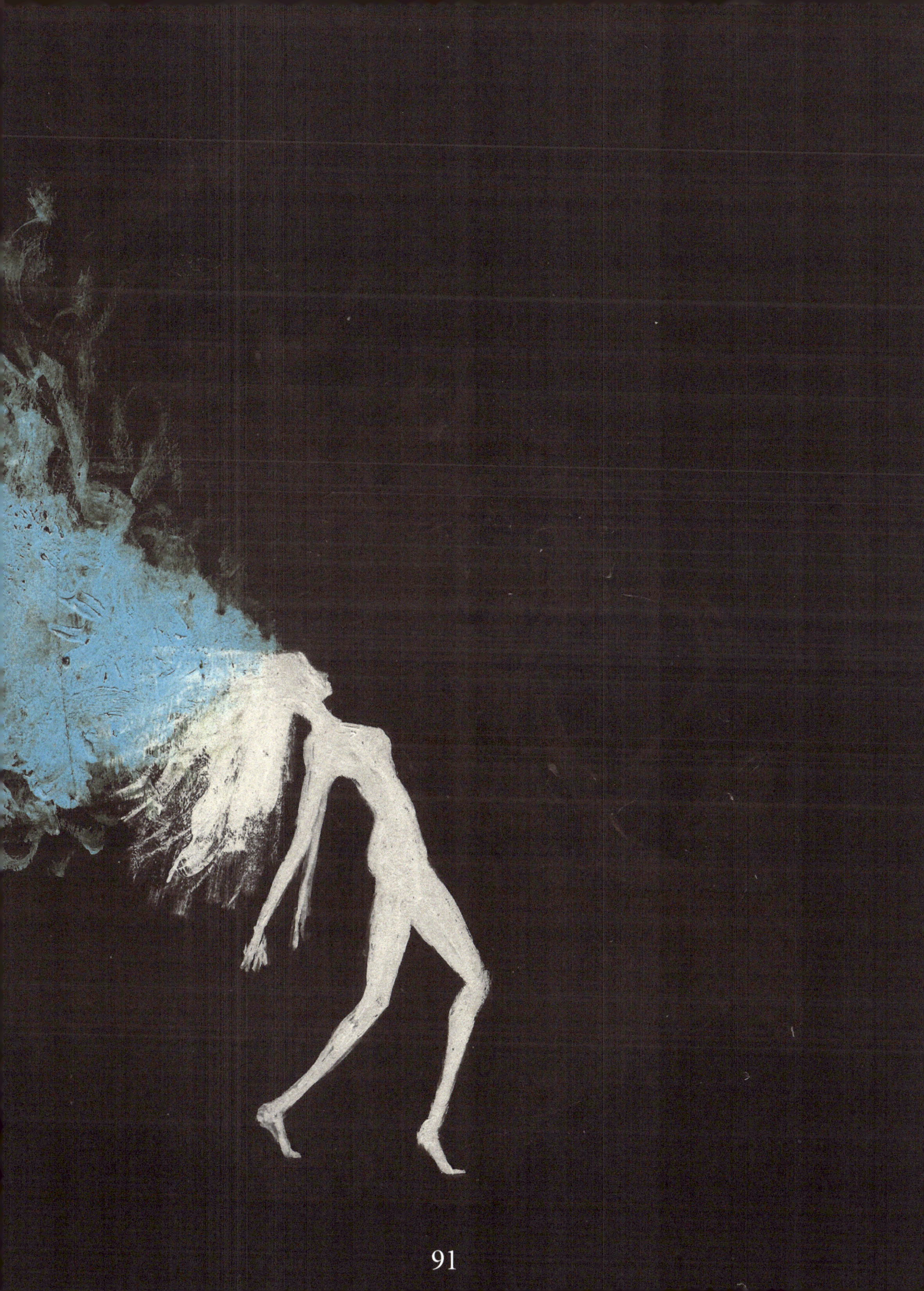

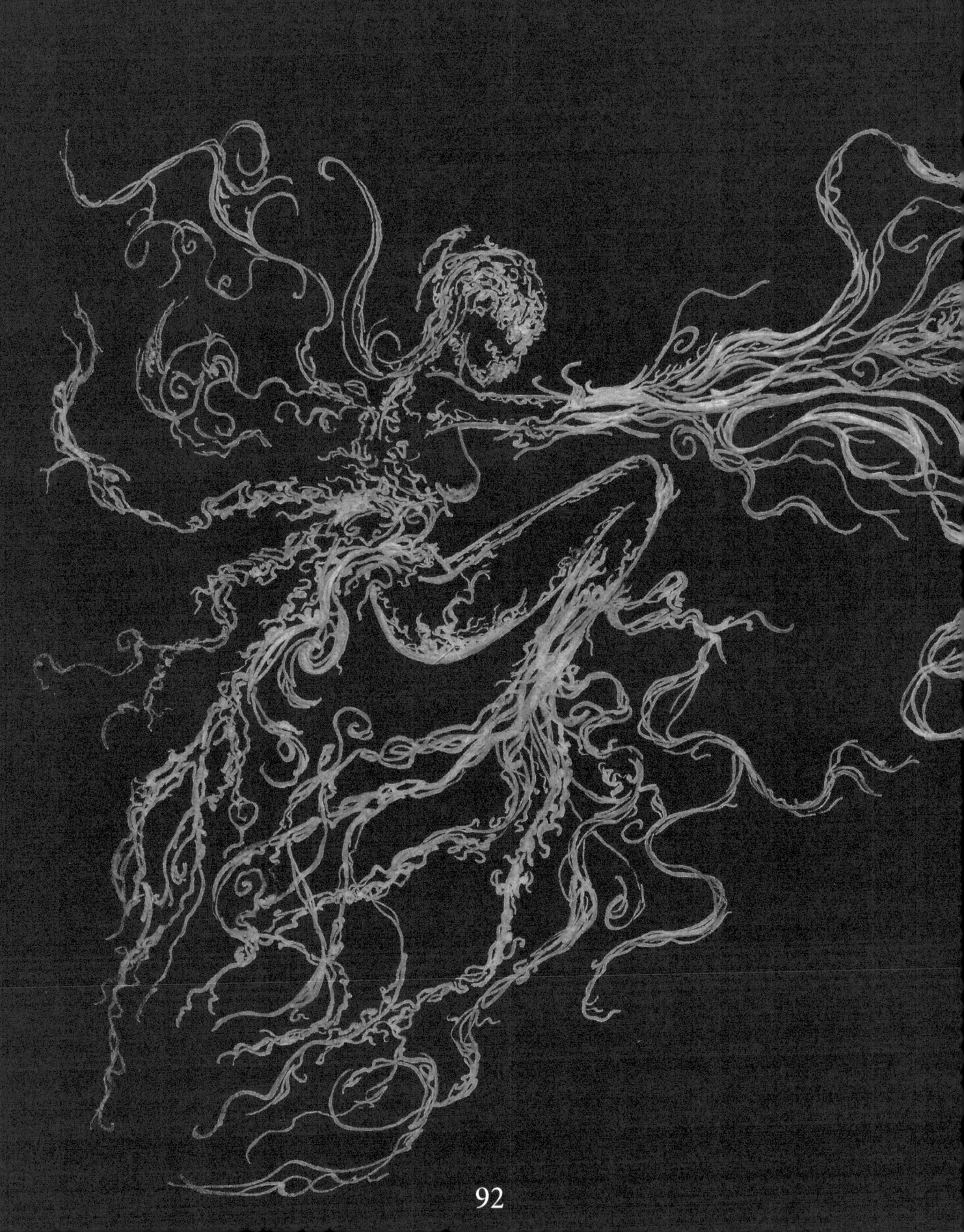

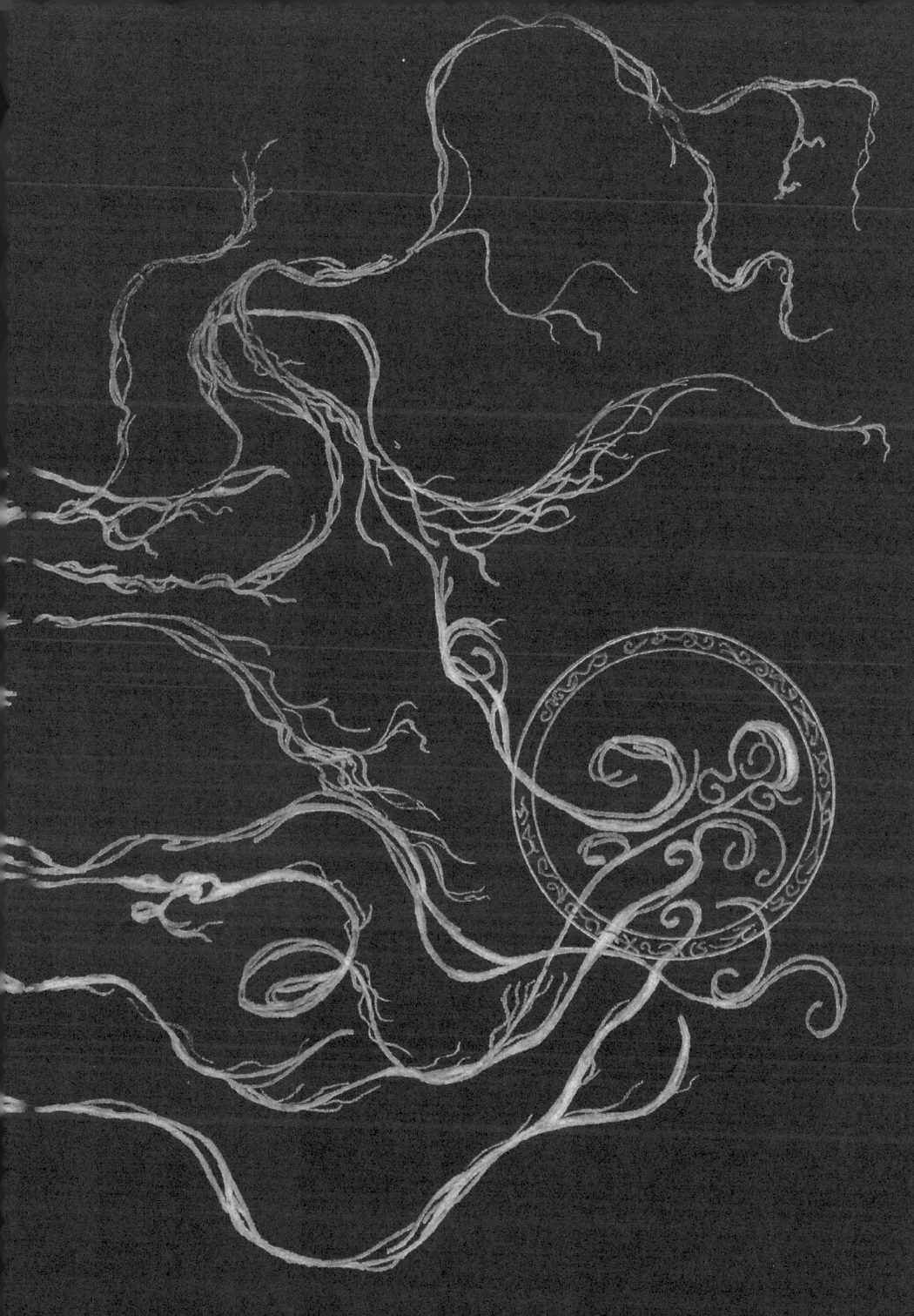

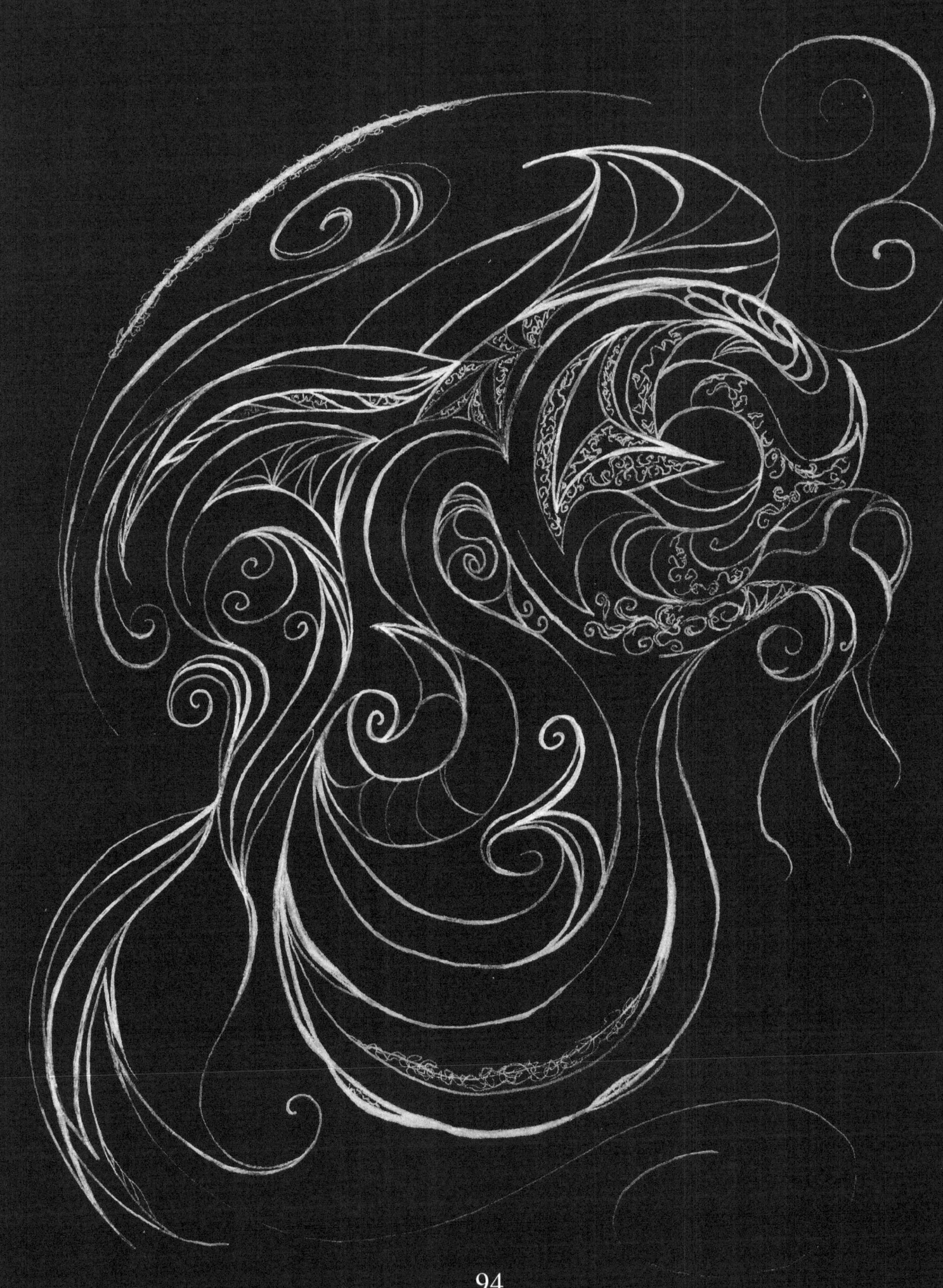

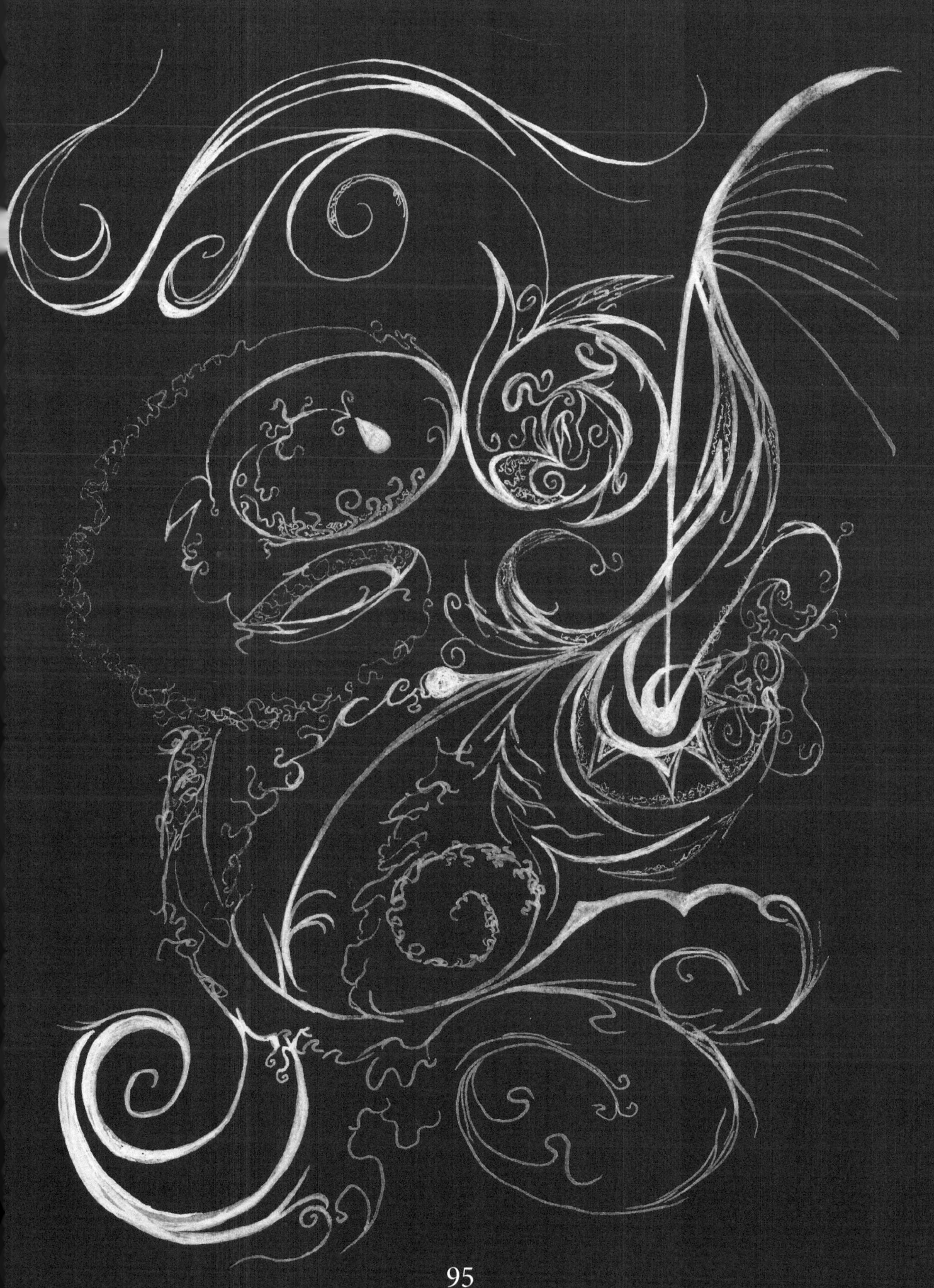

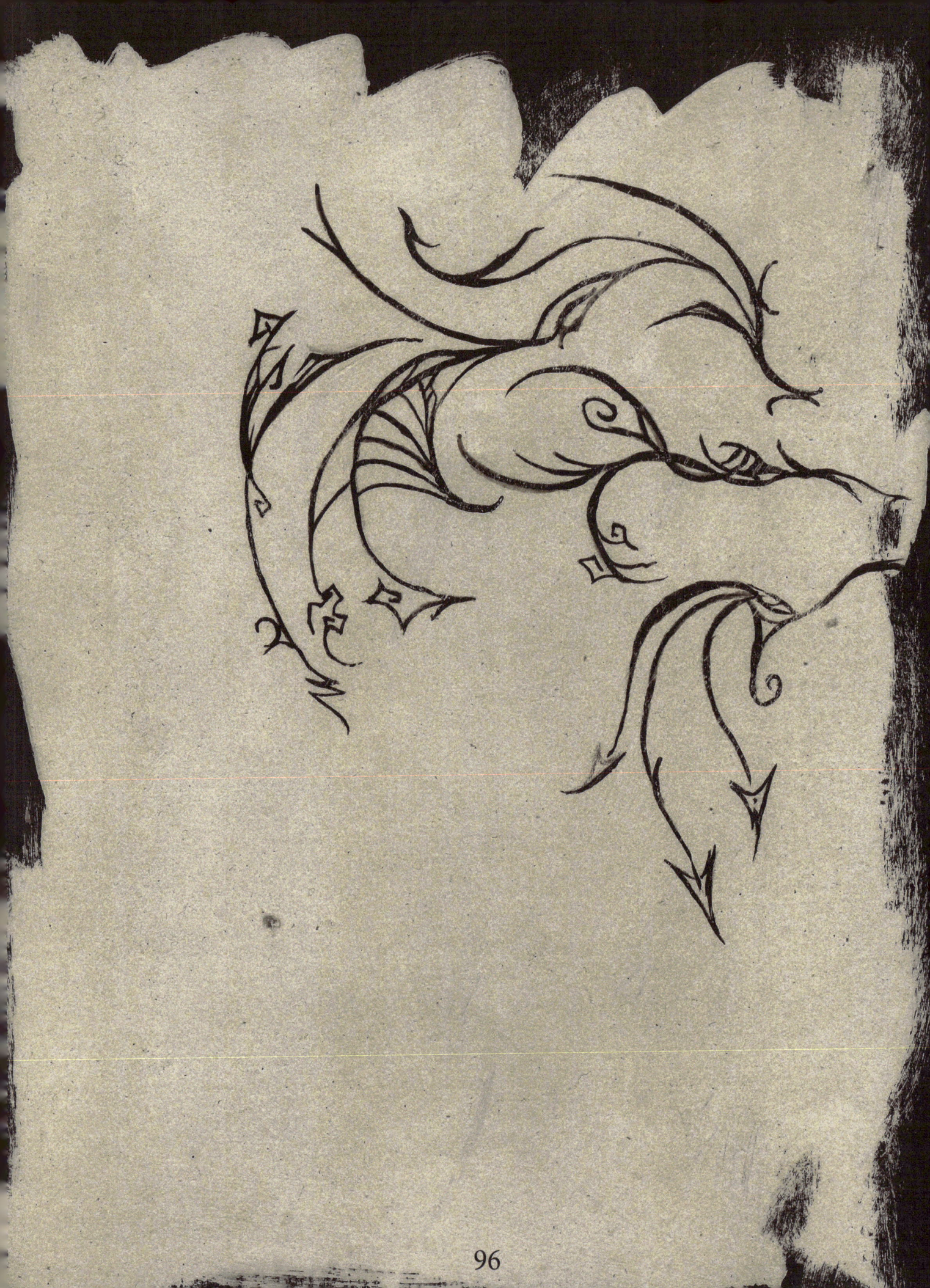

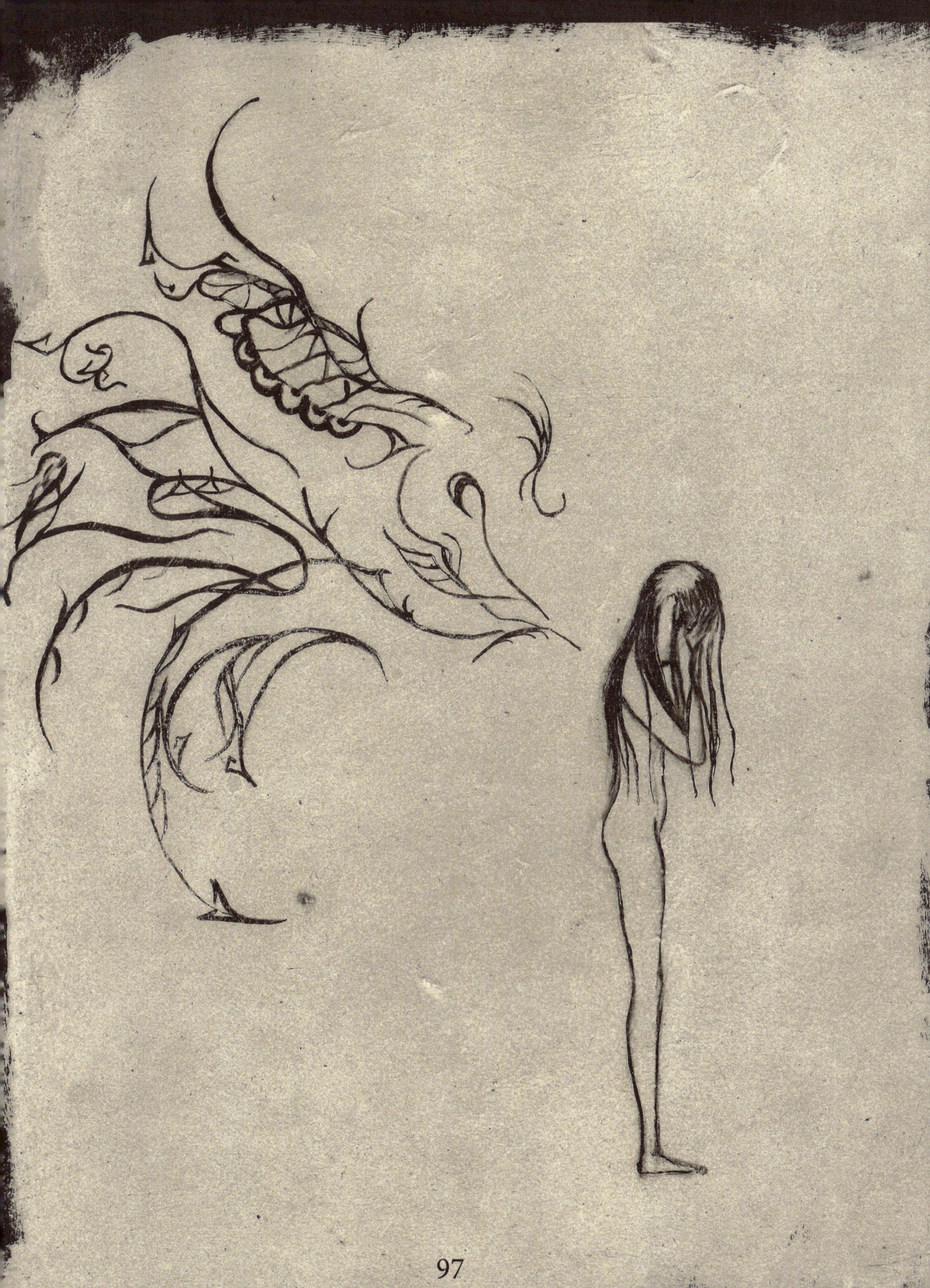

背景情報:

名 .... Markarious
仮名 .... Tobu Heart
出生地 .... Washington, North Carolina. USA
生年月日 1987年1月13日

Back Ground information:
Name .... Markarious
Psuedonym .... Tobu Heart
BirthPlace .... Washington, NC
Date of Birth .... 13 Janauary 1987

連絡先:
ウェブサイト .... TOBUHEART.COM
メール .... TOBUHEART@GMAIL.COM
インスタグラム .... @TOBU HEART

Contact information:
Website .... TOBUHEART.COM
Email .... TOBUHEART@GMAIL.COM
Instagram .... @TOBU HEART